# BARTH

ABINGDON PILLARS
OF THEOLOGY

# BARTH

## EBERHARD BUSCH

Abingdon Press
*Nashville*

BARTH

*This book is printed on acid-free paper.*

Library of Congress Cataloging-in-Publication Data

Busch, Eberhard, 1937-
  Barth / Eberhard Busch.
    p. cm. — (Abingdon Pillars of theology series)
  Includes bibliographical references and index.
  ISBN 978-0-687-49246-6 (binding : pbk., adhesive lay-flat : alk. paper)
  1. Barth, Karl, 1886-1968. I. Title.

  BX4827.B3B845 2008
  230'.044092—dc22

                                                                        2007030232

08 09 10 11 12 13 14 15 16 17—10 9 8 7 6 5 4 3 2 1

MANUFACTURED IN THE UNITED STATES OF AMERICA

# CONTENTS

# TRANSLATORS' PREFACE

The majority of references in this volume are to Barth's *Church Dogmatics*. We have provided the volume numbers and pages within parentheses throughout this text. After the volume number (for example, IV/1), the first page number refers to the original German edition (*Kirchliche Dogmatik*) followed by [=] and the page number of the English edition (*Church Dogmatics*). The abbreviation "rev." indicates a revision of the English translation (ET). We have tried to render Barth's German into English as accurately and yet as clearly as possible. At the same time, we have also tried to respect the current conventions of inclusive language. Following the practice of Darrell and Judith Guder as stated in the translators' preface of Karl Barth's *The Theology of the Reformed Confessions* (Louisville: Westminster John Knox Press, 2002), "Wherever we could do so and both remain true to the original and produce readable English, we have rendered *Mensch* with 'human, person, humanity' and used 'one' to translate the German impersonal pronoun *man*. We have followed the German original in the gender of pronouns [for example, the church is referred to as 'she'] and in language of deity." Where the term "man" appears within previously translated texts and elsewhere, it is to be understood generically. We are grateful for the author's friendship and for his ready help in answering our questions along the way, but any translation errors are definitely ours and not his.

Richard and Martha Burnett live in Due West, South Carolina, where Richard teaches at Erskine Theological Seminary and Martha is a homemaker.

# INTRODUCTION

Editors of the magazine *Der Spiegel* once gathered to have a conversation with Karl Barth regarding a cover story written about him. They explained to him that the article should have the title, "God's Partisan." Barth remarked, "It would be better to write 'God's *Cheerful* Partisan.'" And so it was. That title is a summary description of both Karl Barth, the person, and his lasting contribution to theology.

Barth was indeed a fighter, especially against stupidity and wrong thinking. But he also wrote in one of his greatest works: "One is either a theologian with joy or not a theologian at all. Sullen faces, morose thoughts and boring expressions cannot be tolerated at all, especially in this science" (II/1, 740 = 656, rev.). He fought for troubled people and oppressed truths. Yet he was a theologian who listened daily to the music of Wolfgang Amadeus Mozart before he began his work. The light that he saw, while he heard this music, helped him see the darkness in which people suffered, and, at the same time, this light helped him see a great hope for them.

Karl Barth was born in Basel, Switzerland, May 10, 1886, and died there December 10, 1968. But what a rich, inspired, and inspiring life took place between these two dates. Barth was on the move all his life, inwardly as well as outwardly. He was someone who could work hard yet enjoy life, someone who tore down but also built up, and someone who comforted others yet got angry. In these ways, he was typical. Yet he also listened, instructed, admonished, and continually called upon his contemporaries to meet the challenges of the day with careful and courageous responsibility. In these ways he was extraordinary. We get a glimpse of the secret of his resolve in one of his last lectures, "In theological science, continuation always means 'beginning once again at the beginning.'"[1]

The richness of his life and work is closely connected with the motto he sought to follow. What really matters is "to say the same thing again and again in different words." By this he did not mean that we are always to say again and again something different, nor did he mean that we are to say the same thing over and over. But our question is how did he undertake to say the same thing again and again in different words? Or what made his way of always beginning at the begin-ning significant for his theology?

One way, though not the primary one, was based on his ability to give himself afresh to new times and new conversations with different people in different sit-uations with their particular challenges. But more decisively, his inspiration came from the truth of the "eternally bounteous God" as goes one of his favorite hymns. Karl Barth's theology is particularly characterized by being in and remaining in constant movement and transformation. According to Barth, Christians have to take this truth seriously in their actions and speech as well as in their hearing and thinking. As they do so, they will walk a path in which the same thing will be expressed again and again *differently*; yet, again and again it will be *the same thing*. By this he means that in walking this path the Christian must exercise self-correction in order to learn how to live out the same thing again and again in a better and more appropriate way.

Karl Barth's life can be divided into three periods. Each will be discussed under a phrase that was typical for Barth at the time and that characterizes the under-lying content of his theology. Later I will introduce some of the central insights from his most important work, the *Church Dogmatics*.

# CHAPTER 1

# THE EARLY PERIOD OF BARTH'S THEOLOGY: "GOD IS GOD"

G od is God." This is a core sentence from *the* book that first gained Barth notoriety and opposition but also applause far beyond the borders of his native Switzerland.[1] In 1921, Barth was in his tenth year as pastor in the industrial village, Safenwil. This book, *Der Römerbrief*, is an exegesis of the apostle Paul's Letter to the Romans. The title is provocative because it indicates that Barth does not want to understand *Paul* but wants to understand who God is and what God says *with* Paul. The book is full of radical insights and subversive formulations. After hearing one of Barth's sermons, the young novelist Manfred Hausmann wrote, "I was gripped and uprooted, and then turned inside out . . . I left the church as one who no longer knew where to go. Lightning had . . . come down and struck me. I was staggering. Here was the revolution I had suspected all along."[2]

Barth's insights launched what is called dialectical theology. It stood in contrast to previous theological lines—to liberal theology, as represented by his teachers Adolf von Harnack and Wilhelm Herrmann, as well as to its conservative counterpart, as represented by his teachers Adolf Schlatter and Theodor Haering. The expression *dialectical theology* is derived from its method of thinking in unresolved contrasts. As Barth explained in one of his lectures: we *should* talk about God, but we *cannot* talk about God; therefore, we have to say *both* of these things and give God the glory.

It is precisely within Barth's *Römerbrief* that we repeatedly come across this strange statement, God is God. This kind of phrase is called a tautology, that is, a sentence that looks like an explanation but really does not explain anything. For example, if I want to know what a candle is, I am not really helped if I am informed that a candle is a candle. Why then this sentence: "God is God"? What does it say about God and about Barth as a theologian?

In order to understand, we have to go back a little further. From 1909 to 1911, Barth was an assistant pastor in Geneva, where he preached most of his sermons from John Calvin's old pulpit. This, however, did not stop him from speaking out as a devout disciple of the neo-Protestantism of his time, which was fundamentally shaped by liberal theology. This theology held that its source was in the inherent religious capacities of human beings, not in God's revelation, which is given by the grace of God to real sinners. Barth continued to speak this way when he became the pastor in the village of Safenwil. From the beginning his speech was noticeably filled with a deep love for Jesus. "He was the greatest of all to whom it was given to reveal the mystery of life for others."[3] But for Barth the meaning of this love is embedded in the thought world of neo-Protestantism, and his most important model for this was Friedrich Schleiermacher (1768–1834).

His reliance on Schleiermacher is clear in his interpretation of the figure of this "Jesus." In one of his sermons, Barth says, "I openly admit that I . . . would have no interest in Jesus" if we were to understand him "according to the formulas of old church doctrine."[4] But it is not only the Jesus of church dogma but also the historical Jesus that is "not the foundation of our faith." "Faith does not mean to accept with your mind . . . that everything you have heard is truth."[5] To know who Jesus "really" is can only happen "by an experience."[6] An "experience" in this case refers to an event along the lines of the verse by the seventeenth-century mystic Angelus Silesius: "If Christ were born a thousand times in Bethlehem yet not in you, then you would still be lost eternally."[7] This is what Barth calls, along with Friedrich Schleiermacher, the "true" revelation.[8]

But during these years, Barth suddenly began speaking about Jesus in a quite reserved way. Jesus is not God.[9] He is "our way to the Father."[10] Often when Barth referred to the experience of "the inner life of Jesus," he meant that "the same thing that happened in Jesus happens in us." Thus, "The power and life that you sense in him can become your power and life."[11] And if we humble ourselves obediently we are then doing "the same that Jesus did and, together with him, we go from death to life."[12] This is what took place in the first disciples of Jesus. On the "basis of their impression of Jesus' person and way, their own inner life" grew.[13] And "as you attempt to go through your Good Fridays in his way, you will experience Easter with him."[14]

But Barth's thinking, molded by liberal theology, began to change in Safenwil. It simply had to take a backseat to his work on the social problems people were facing there. Historically the village of Safenwil had belonged to an area once governed by the so-called gracious Lords of Bern. Unfortunately, these same lords took undue advantage of the people. The local pastors were also controlled by these lords and were under oath to serve them as collectors of tribute for Bern. The pastor served as a kind of village judge. Habitually, after the sermon, court was set up in church under a painting of the bear of Bern. Sluggards, grumblers, and single mothers were punished or put in a jail right beside the manse. Although the pastors certainly had to preach also, their sermons often only served as moral reinforcement of the system. This kind of governance was kept up until after Napoleon removed the Lords of Bern from their office and separated the area of Aargau from the canton of Bern. During Barth's time, however, two factory owners ruled Safenwil. The custom was that after reaching confirmation age (between fourteen and sixteen years old), boys and girls went to work in the factories. Both male and female workers worked more than twelve hours a day and earned hardly enough for a meager living.

One of the factory owners who had "donated" the manse thought that it was the role of the pastor to see to it that people were content with their fate and limited prospects. But this calculation did not quite work in Karl Barth's case. He was not the sort of pastor easily coerced, especially when the lives of his parishioners were involved. One of the factory owners even left the church and, since he did not want to miss out on religion, founded a religious club.

This new pastor was the first one in a long time who was on the side of the poor and oppressed. They did not call Barth "Pastor," but "Comrade Pastor." He lived with them in "solidarity," a word that he also began using in church. His opponents and detractors, however, called him "the red pastor" after he became a member of the Social Democratic Party, which was highly unusual for a pastor. Barth trained workers to fight for their rights by living in solidarity with one another, and he became an advocate for female factory workers, who were especially disadvantaged. In all this he kept in contact with Swiss "religious socialism" (Leonhard Ragaz, 1868–1945). In this movement, Christians became members of the socialistic party in their hope of God's promise to renew the whole world.

Yet, in all these activities, Barth did not neglect his task as *verbi divini* minister, that is, as servant of the Word of God, as it is still called today. He took his tasks so seriously, especially the task of preparing sermons every week, that the Bible began to speak to Barth anew. This was especially the case after 1914 with his deep disappointment with his liberal teachers Harnack and Herrmann and the Social Democratic leaders in Germany who gave their assent to Germany's entrance into World War I. Barth now entered into a deep search and made new discoveries. During this time, he said in a sermon, "What we say is not so important, but rather what is being said to us."[15]

In 1916 he gave a lecture on "The New World of the Bible." What a strange book it is. "The hungry have enough to eat and for those who already have enough it is spoiled before they even open it." "What counts is not the right thoughts of man about God that make up the content of the Bible but the right thoughts of God about man." "The main thing is that we acknowledge once again God as God."[16]

As Barth studied the Epistle to the Romans, it opened up for him, and he began to understand it in an exciting way. Just as the salvation of God had been hidden from the Jews and began to shine among the Gentiles, so this event was being repeated in our times. The salvation of God has been moved far away from *Christians* and has come very near to *non-Christians*. It has become strange to those who know him and is breaking in upon those who do not know him. God is not there where we think we possess him, and he is there where he seems to be absent. Through Jewish-Christian friends, he also got to know Franz Rosenzweig, a Jew, who claimed (as of 1914) that "the distinctiveness between God and man, this terrible offense to all new and old paganism," had to be asserted.

After the first edition of the *Römerbrief* was published, Barth began to completely revise it within ten months. In this second edition, Barth often uses the phrase, "God is God." This statement signals the end of his desire to explain the divine. The statement now functions normatively. Typically when we say, "God is . . ." we usually then add a word that describes something important to *us*. But from this point on, when Barth says, "God is *God*," he does not add another explanation next describing who or what God is. Barth points out that our explanations represent a great danger because "God" is then substituted for something else that *we* have declared to be God. So our explanations, in actuality, turn "God" into an idol of our own making.

First of all, the sentence "God is God" says that we cannot own God. This means that what we can own *never* is God. Wanting to have God at our disposal, frankly, is, for Barth, the greatest sin. And those who claim to know God already are committing this sin. To his last days, Barth taught that part of our sin is that we believe *ourselves* to be free of sin, yet, at the same time, we see it in others. He goes on to say that we believe this because we think that God is on *our* side. But I can only take sin seriously when I recognize it as *my* sin. Barth puts it provocatively in the *Römerbrief*. A sinner—"that's *me*, not the rich man, the sensual man, or the man of power who has to say so of himself. . . . but the one consecrated to God, the man with a . . . genuine religious experience, the prophet, the apostle, the reformer—as even Jesus says about himself: 'Why do you call *me* good? *No one* is good except God alone.' "[17] Barth does not understand this as a reversal wherein bad people get to be on top and good people go to the bottom. Rather, the notion of being on top or bottom is abolished, because through God we have all been placed on the sinner's bench together. Barth uses the term "solidarity" to describe this.

Second, "God is God" says that God is known only through *God*. Barth does not mean simply that God is beyond us or transcendent. He says, "God is *beyond* both 'here' *and* 'there.' "[18] This means that when God is beyond that which is there, he is also here. Or, as Barth says, "God is known as the *unknown* God."[19] But this is not to be understood as if God is hidden from us only at the beginning and then is no longer hidden after he has unveiled himself to us. Rather, it is when God is revealed to us that we are all the more dependent on his unveiling of himself to us. It is clearly not that he falls into our hands. Rather, it is the reverse. We fall into his hands.

Of course, it is God who *reaches* us. He makes himself known to us. But although it is God who reaches us, Barth cannot emphasize strongly enough that he is *unreachable* to us. Revelation, the grace of God, is like an "arrow from the other side of a shore on which *we* will never set foot, yet it hits *us*."[20] For this reason Barth speaks dialectically, that is, in paradoxes such as, "The righteousness of God is a *standing place in the air* which exists outside all other possible or familiar places to stand."[21] Jesus "puts himself even in those places where God can be present only as a question about God."[22] And faith is "a void, a bowing down before that which we will never be, never have, and can never do. It is a bowing down before him who will never become world or man except in the complete negation . . . of all that we here and now call man and world."[23] "Faith is therefore never finished, never merely given, never a secure possession. Psychologically considered, it is always and ever again a leap into uncertainty."[24] Briefly stated, God cannot be grasped by humanity, especially *in* his revelation. We are always absolutely dependent on his revelation to us. Even when God makes himself present on this side, this does not make him into a fact among other facts. "The revelation of Jesus is at the same time the greatest conceivable veiling of God."[25]

Barth stated all of these theological claims rather sharply and one-sidedly. He needed time to reflect on how he would say all this again in a more appropriate way. He had to think through how he could make clear that in his veiling God really does become accessible to us. We should never forget, however, that from his early days, Barth reminded us of what revelation is. He reminded us that when God revealed his name to Moses, "I AM WHO I AM" (Exod 3:14), this revelation of God's name also consists, of course, in a refusal to give his name. And, after all, this is the name by which we too may call upon God and know him!

## Questions for Reflection

1. In his *Römerbrief* Barth says, "God! We do not know what this word means. The one who believes knows that we do not know it."[26] And "God and the man I am—these do *not* go together."[27] Has Barth not stated this too radically and, therefore, not carefully enough? Do these sentences betray a compulsion already in Barth to speak about God even while continuously denying all of humanity's possibilities to do so?

2. Is the Roman Catholic theologian Hans Urs von Balthasar right when he says with respect to the *Römerbrief*, "Barth's cry: 'Not I! Rather God!' actually directs all eyes on itself instead of on God."[28] Does this sentence say the same thing as God and *evil*, or God and *sin*, do not go together? Or, if he is not saying

the same thing, what is the difference? Or, to put it another way, a frequent objection against Barth in his *Römerbrief* period is that he taught that God can do everything and humanity can do nothing. Yet we certainly also read in his *Römerbrief*, grace does not mean that humanity "can and should do nothing. Grace means that *God* is doing something. [And] grace does not mean that God does 'everything' [which would then mean that humanity would not have anything to do], but [grace means that God] is doing something very specific."[29] And this "grace is also sufficient for ethics."[30] What do you think?

# CHAPTER 2

# THE RISE OF THE CONFESSING CHURCH: "THE ONE WORD OF GOD"

T he One Word of God"—delegates of the Protestant churches in Germany adopted these words as part of a church confession on May 31, 1934, during a synod meeting in Wuppertal-Barmen. It was about a year after the National Socialists had seized power in Germany. The newspaper of the German town Wuppertal in the Rhine-District, for once uncensored, reported on this meeting under the headline, "An Historic Church Event."

Delegates of the Protestant churches in Germany had been sent to the synod and the document that was eventually issued was called The Theological Declaration of Barmen 1934, or the Barmen Declaration. In opposition to the growing conformity of the German Evangelical Church to the Nazi state, this declaration established the Confessing Church. For the first time since the Reformation, Lutheran, United, and Reformed representatives of the Protestant churches confessed the faith together. And what they confessed together was not merely the opinion of one group voicing its opinion among others in the church. The assertion of the text was highly significant, so much so that those who did not join in affirming it would find themselves *outside* the Protestant church. Here *the* church of Jesus Christ speaks.

Three theologians were elected to prepare the text of the Declaration. But while the other two took an afternoon nap, Karl Barth, alone, wrote this text. Thus he was the primary drafter of the Theological Declaration. At the time, he put his theological knowledge entirely into the service of the church, and representatives of the churches accepted this service. Several churches outside of Germany, for example, in the United States and Cuba, later formally affirmed this confession.

Today some people see it as a great failure that churches did not directly criticize Hitler's regime. They accuse these churches of thinking, once again, only of themselves and simply allowing the world to be the world. Such criticism is obviously a misunderstanding. It must be remembered that the churches at that time were already highly politicized, having given their assent, for the most part, to this regime. Hitler had no reason at all to fear any criticism from the church. One part of the church was seeking to transport national ideology into its structure. That was the group known as the German Christians. Another part, the Pastors' Emergency League, wanted to keep politics out of the pulpit, but they affirmed National Socialistic rule within the realm of the state. At Barmen there were mainly representatives of this latter group. But in the Barmen Declaration, these representatives now engaged in an act of *repentance* and acknowledged that their understanding of the situation up to this point had been wrong. The change is obvious in that the theses of Barmen contain "something" entirely different from the various other confessions of 1933. This was clear to everyone at that time. It was characteristic of the many confessions of 1933 that, regardless from which side they were written, they all generally began with a confessional-sounding word in which the church praised God for Adolf Hitler's rise to power with his German national, antidemocratic ideology. At least representatives of the Pastors' Emergency League went on *after that* to talk about God and of his Christ.

In 1933, Karl Barth had already written to address this second group, "The presupposition—as though one were in agreement with the preamble of the 'German Christians' [with respect to the church's approval of Hitler's authority]—that anxiously endeavors not to let others be more zealous in this preamble while disregarding all that is happening to the Jews right now—so that in opposition to [the German Christians] one can have a pure church, will prove to be one of the worst illusions in an age full of illusions. Once and for all, let us drop the preamble, straightforwardly and entirely, which is basically the confession of a world-historical, political party, and after that we will talk further about what comes next."[1]

As strange as it may sound, what was provocative about the Barmen Declaration was simply that it dropped any such preamble. The *first* thesis gives specific and detailed reasons for this. It begins by citing the order of the Evangelical Church in Germany at the time: "Jesus Christ, as He is attested in Holy Scripture" and then come the five new and all-decisive words: "*is the one Word of God.*"[2]

The Barmen Declaration does not mean that God has spoken only once. Nor does it contradict Hebrews 1:1-2, "Long ago God spoke to our ancestors in many and various ways by the prophets, but in these last days he has spoken to us by [his] Son." The speaking of this one Word of God instead says that there is no other binding Word of God for Christians other than the one spoken to us by the God who is united with us in Jesus Christ. He speaks ever and again *differently* to us and to others. But we have to follow *no other* God than the one attested to us in Holy Scripture. Just as we have been justified by grace alone, as the Reformation explained, so in the same way the Barmen Declaration now says that we have to follow God alone. Basically, this is a vigorous insistence upon the absolute validity of the first commandment as expressed in the Bible. "I am the LORD your God, who brought you out of the land of Egypt, out of the house of slavery; you shall have no other gods before me" (Exod 20:1-3).

Barth had earlier explained, "There is today a disagreement within the church regarding matters of the first commandment and we have to 'confess' that today."[3] Later in 1946, when he sat across from the future leader of East Berlin, Walter Ulbricht, he reminded him of this very first commandment. The emphasis on it *is* a central concern in Karl Barth's theology.

Yet Barth used to say that only the *consequences* show how something was meant. He drew a number of consequences from what was said at Barmen. Four of them are listed here. The *first* consequence has to do with the understanding of what the Bible calls the *law* of God. Barth felt compelled to think about this in a new way because at that time many prominent German theologians, also his former friend Friedrich Gogarten, understood God's law as a hostile power against the gospel that is free of all law. This made the law of God look the same as all the hard claims of the authorities, for example, Hitler's dictatorship. Whoever obeys them does not do anything wrong. Whoever does not obey them is punished by the authorities and rightly so. The gospel on the other hand is considered to be free from all of God's commands. His grace can only be received in pure passivity. It *cannot* contain any command and certainly not one that would call for resistance to the orders of the authorities. Barth now opened up a new chapter in this matter as he read Holy Scripture.

He was also concerned with what was said in the *second* thesis of the Barmen Declaration that the one Word of God has two forms: consolation and claim. Barth does not mean that these are two different things but that both of them are connected. It also means that God's grace is costly and not cheap. God's grace is imperious, and God's law is merciful. So our passivity is not in accord with his grace, but our active response is. And so Barth writes that the love of God "does not want to rule over puppets and slaves but rather in the triumph of the free decision of faithful servants and friends" (II/2, 195f. = 178f., rev.). According to Barth, when we obey the laws of the state we are not necessarily obeying God as well. Christians certainly have to take earthly orders seriously, but the divine command allows us to test human commands as to whether they are in accord with the wholesome will of God.

Barth pointed to the words of Jesus in Matthew 6:24: "You cannot serve God and mammon" (I/2, 74; IV/2, 189; IV/3, 960). It was important for him to see that, above all, the difference between "serving *God*" and "mammon" does not merely mean that one should serve the one instead of the other. The difference between these two is clearly recognizable since obedience to God has its own character compared to obedience to earthly rules. He writes about this in his *Dogmatics*: "The command of God sets man free. The command of God permits. It is only in this way that it commands. This is the case because the command . . . is itself the form of the grace of God—the *easy* yoke and the *light* burden of Christ, . . . which as such are not to be exchanged for any other yoke or burden, and the assumption of which is in every sense our *quickening* and *refreshing*" (II/2, 650f. = 586).

The *second* consequence of the Barmen Declaration is the discovery of the indissoluble bond of Christians with *Jews*. At the time, Christians *usually* saw Jews as members of a foreign religion, a foreign race, or as a people rejected by God. The Barmen Declaration's statement about Christ as the "*one* Word of God" sets forth a new position on this issue. It represents a New Testament exegesis of the Old Testament's first commandment: "I am the LORD your God, who brought you out of the land of Egypt, out of the house of slavery; you shall have no other gods before me" (Exod 20:1-3).

Barth's first theological statement after Hitler's "seizure of power" was actually his lecture on "The First Commandment as a Theological Axiom" in which he explains all this.[4] And during an Advent sermon in 1933, he explained, after speaking on Romans 15, that, first, the Son of God has taken on Jewish flesh and blood, and he did so in such a way that we who come from other ethnic groups are standing before closed doors in contrast to these people. Second, preference for the Jews before all other peoples lies within God's good pleasure, as does making a covenant with them out of free grace and not according to their ability to do good. Thus, the covenant can never be broken. Therefore, whoever is against the Jews is against God's free grace. Third, John 4:22—a verse that became, through Barth's influence, the confession of the Protestant relief organization of Switzerland during World War II—"Salvation is from the Jews." This means that the Jewish people are opening the closed door for us in that they have simply treated Christ as all others would have done. But because God does not reject them, his goodness is extended to us as well who are Gentiles and even greater sinners. And fourth, out of this abundant grace for Jews and Gentiles comes the clear command, "Accept each other." Barth boldly says that Jesus "sees us as Jews arguing with the *true* God"—which is the true meaning of *Israel*—and he sees us "as gentiles at peace with the *false* gods, but he sees us both as 'children of the living God'" who "can only shake hands with one another."[5]

Barth sent this sermon immediately to Adolf Hitler with a letter saying that he should learn what the Christian church is really about. At the time, Barth wrote an epilogue to that same sermon, "because of faith in Christ, who was himself a Jew, it is simply not right to join in the disdain and cruelty toward Jews which has become the order of the day."[6]

A *third* consequence is the matter of taking seriously what the *community of Jesus Christ* is. Amid all the criticisms of his *Römerbrief*, Barth was affected most by Adolf Schlatter's question, "Are we then . . . isolated, lonely 'readers' who have long forgotten that we are members of the church?" The 1920s had already brought about a new discovery of this topic in Germany. Otto Dibelius' book *The Century of the Church* was typical. But for Barth the title of this book lacked clarity. And during the 1930s, it became obvious how easily a church so proud of herself could be led astray. Barth tried to bring clarity by using the phrase "The Church must be *the Church*." She may neither be a hidden monastery nor a department store. And he worked hard to get this point across. He did so out of the conviction that the *church herself* is her own greatest threat and that she must resist this threat above all others. He regarded Dietrich Bonhoeffer's idea of leaving the church because of the infiltration of Nazi ideology as an unhelpful escape from this task. He insisted that *you*, the followers of this ideology, have left the church. Part of the significance of the Barmen Declaration was that it called those in error back to the church. Therefore, he called those resisting this error the Confessing Church.

But for Barth the church is in order when Christ *alone* is at her center and when her members are no more and no less than brothers and sisters, according to Barmen's *third* and *fourth* theses. The title of "brother" used in the third thesis refers to Jewish Christians, who the German Christians were trying to force out of the church. This new insight Barth gained in his knowledge of the church is reflected in his new primary work, begun in 1932. Its title was no longer like its precursor of the 1920s, *Christian Dogmatics*. Such a title might suggest a person thinking about the meaning of the term *Christian* by *oneself*, from a merely academic perspective. Barth called this new work the *Church Dogmatics* to show that the theological task was now quite consciously in service of the church. The *sixth* thesis of the Barmen Declaration declares that sending missionaries to all nations is one of the essential tasks of the church and that this task must not be restricted by racial limits.

A *fourth* consequence is one that Barth described during lectures he gave in Scotland in 1938 with the bold phrase, "political service of God."[7] This does not mean a divine blessing is claimed for any political or warlike endeavor done in one's own strength. When Barth writes in June of 1933 that it is really a matter today of pursuing theology "as if nothing had happened," he adds that this statement includes "indirectly, even politics."[8]

Barth does not mean indifference toward politics. As the passage further indicates, Christians should not allow foreign powers to dictate their political judgments. They are to obey God rather than people (see Acts 5:29). According to the Barmen Declaration's *fifth* thesis, political service of God is about the maintenance and protection of "justice and peace," about righteousness and public welfare in the common life of humanity, and according to the best human judgment. Such service of God takes place where this is *done* and not where politicians simply call themselves Christians. This kind of action is also called service of God because Christians may trust that God "upholds the universe by the word of His power" (see Heb 1:3), whatever else human beings may accomplish, well or not so well in this regard. Christians, therefore, can be politically active without compromising their faith. If they are true to their faith, this must show itself in their commitment to justice and public welfare. That they do so as Christians should not be said, rather it should be *noticed*, as Barth used to say, according to Matthew 7:16.

If not all, then at least most members of the Barmen synod knew about Barth's meeting with 150 pastors of the Pastors' Emergency League on October 31, 1933, in Berlin. It was there that he tried to explain to them that once the church understands that indeed she cannot serve *two* masters, God *and* a worldly power, she will not cease to be put into the world of such powers, but she will be put there *differently*. And then it may become, quite concretely, "very dangerous." For she will then finally ask, "What has happened this summer in Germany? Did it happen justly or unjustly? What about this kind of seizure of power? What about the liquidation of all other parties? What about the confiscation of property? What took place in the concentration camps? What happened to the Jews? Can Germany, can the German Church, accept responsibility for so many suicides? Has the Church not also become guilty in all this by keeping silent? Whoever proclaims the Word of God has to speak what the Word of God says about such actions."[9]

Barth was immediately expelled from Germany for these statements. Nevertheless, what is important about them is this: wherever the church *looses* herself from any bond which is to God's Word *and at the same time* to worldly power, wherever she listens *solely* to God's Word, she will not cease to speak out politically, but she will do so from a *different* position.

But with respect to justice and peace, there is the borderline case of war. This borderline case became real for Barth in 1939. Peace, he said, is only true peace when it is a just peace. If a system of injustice is hidden beneath the cloak of peace, war can be waged for the sake of a just peace. In his lectures and writings, he defended his conviction that the German military was waging an unjust war of destruction against humanity and that, by all means, for the sake of Germany's future, it must be resisted. As a sign of his resolve he enrolled at the age of fifty-four as a soldier in the Swiss Army. In open letters to non-German foreign countries, he wrote that the risen Lord says,

> All power has been given to me in Heaven and on earth . . . Everything we speak out against today regarding the murder of nations and Jews by Germany stands or falls with the truth of this word. Therefore all powers on earth are limited. Therefore his servants may neither give up nor give way in the midst of the present turmoil. Therefore they may not in the midst of this turmoil become ivory tower thinkers and come "in the name of some human ideal" or start a crusade against godless evil. Therefore they must soberly reject injustice, knowing that it is simply about "defending justice . . . against fundamental injustice." [10]

# Questions for Reflection

1. How does Barth's statement about the "one Word of God" relate to his earlier statement "God is God"? Is there progress here with respect to the theology of his *Römerbrief* period? What remained the same in all this?

2. How does talk about the "one Word of God" relate to the distinction between the "two forms of the one Word"? Is there actually a real difference? Is the gospel not then obscured by its connection with the law of God? And is the law of God not then downplayed by its connection with the gospel?

3. Barth sees the Old and the New Testament (the first commandment of Exodus 20:1-3 and "Christ alone") as very closely related. Thus, he could say in March of 1933: "Jesus Christ is the meaning of the law of Sinai."[11] Does this confuse the Old and the New Testaments or are their differences minimized? Are Christians here not simply seizing the first commandment for themselves and snatching it away from the Jewish people? Or how might such an appropriation of the law and, specifically, the first commandment still be asserted in a theologically legitimate way?

4. How can that which Barth calls "political service of God" be distinguished from the spread of evil that occurs when political enterprises use religion to justify their deeds and misdeeds, as most do? Are the concepts of "justice and peace" in the fifth thesis of the Barmen Declaration adequate to describe the political task of "justice and peace"?

CHAPTER 3

# THE THEOLOGIAN IN THE STRUGGLES AND HOPES OF HIS TIME: "NOT ONLY YOUR LOVED ONES!"

"Not only your loved ones!" Let me clarify the situation in which this strange sentence was spoken. When Barth was old, he always treasured conversations with small or large groups of people who wanted to discuss with him topics that were on their hearts. On one such occasion a lady asked him, "Herr Professor, can I be sure that I will see my loved ones in heaven?" He spontaneously replied, "To be sure, you will see *not only* your 'loved ones'!"[1] This story is typical of Barth. It shows his humor, his pugnacious spirit, his unique character as a joyful partisan, his vigilant, lightning-quick reaction, and his friendly correction of a question put the wrong way. It also shows his great hope for humanity and, specifically, for outcasts and forgotten ones. Yet, for Barth, this hope is not based on a sunny disposition such that those who are skeptical or depressed must go without such hope. According to Barth, this hope is based on the great act of God in his creation, namely, in his covenant with his creatures, which was accomplished by him who reconciled those who were once alienated from him.

At this point we need to look more closely at what Barth teaches about such hope and theological knowledge in general in his magnum opus, the *Church Dogmatics*. He delivered the contents of these volumes as lectures at the University of Bonn from 1932 to 1934 and at the University of Basel from 1935 until 1962.

Nearly ten thousand pages in length, these lectures were printed in thirteen thick volumes. At that time people whispered that God let Barth live so long because the angels could hardly wait to see what all this man would put down on paper. The secret of his productive creativity, according to his own opinion, lies in the fact that a theologian "cannot live today in any way on the interest from a capital amassed yesterday. His only possible procedure every day, in fact every hour, is to begin anew at the beginning."[2] Barth was not quite finished with his *Church Dogmatics* when he stopped writing at the age of seventy-six.

For some people "dogmatics" sounds repulsively like strict rules about things Christians must hold as true, much like the German expression: "Eat, bird, or die."[3] Yet this is not the case with the *Church Dogmatics*. It begins by saying that its instruction is about how the service of witness to God's Word, by word and deed, is being achieved in today's church. On one hand, this instruction is not easy because it asks questions while looking and discussing themes from different perspectives and because it offers new perspectives on those themes. On the other hand, such instruction is not difficult. After all, many lay people have gained a lot by reading the *Church Dogmatics*. At every point, it tries to keep the whole of the Christian faith before the reader's eyes, always speaking about the whole with specific concreteness. "Generalities are dangerous" was one of Barth's favorite phrases (II/2, 51 = 48). For Barth, theology "is the most beautiful of all the sciences" (II/1, 740 = 656), yet it also has "logic." When asked about the significance of reason, he simply replied, "I use it."[4]

And what is reason used for? Barth says that just as Philip asked the Ethiopian official in Acts 8 whether he understood what he was reading, so one can also ask, "Do you understand what you are believing?" Theology seeks to help us *understand* what we read and believe. In theology, as Barth conceives it, one walks a path on which we follow not a principle but a person, Christ; and theology is about following Jesus Christ, following him in the realm of thinking. The Word of God that comes to us in Christ is not simply printed in a book.

The Word of God is a *person, this* person in whom the Word of God is embodied, according to John 1:14. Barth writes, "I had come a long way (or round a detour!) before I began to see better and better that the saying in John 1:14 is the center and the theme of all theology and indeed is really the whole of theology in a nutshell."[5] This is why Barth was called a "Christocentric thinker." Indeed he was, though he never denied that God reveals himself in nature and history. But he insisted that reconciliation through Christ is the standard by which we may know whether, in such places where we think we see him, we are truly dealing with God or with an illusion or even a demon. Jesus Christ is the standard because God revealed *himself* through him, as John 1 tells us. This is certainly not the only place God has revealed himself, but the entire Bible bears decisive witness to this place. And it is precisely this very witness, the witness of the one Word of God, Jesus Christ as he is attested for us in Holy Scripture, that wants to be heard and shall be heard anew by Christians of all times as a Word that speaks with continual validity. This is key to Barth's dogmatics. And because he listened so intently to this Word, his dogmatics became so expansive.

Barth understood Jesus Christ as the fulfillment of a covenant established by God with humanity, as the gracious and absolute yes of the benevolent God. The divine affirmation is given to God's creature, who is threatened by nothingness because of its own guilt.

The highlight of the *Church Dogmatics* is probably the fourth volume (II/2), Barth's doctrine of election, which was written in 1940–41, during the height of Hitler's power. The political context of the time provides a good illustration of the content of Barth's thinking as he applied it to this doctrine. In the face of such an absolute ruler who was spreading himself out and stepping over people with seemingly almighty and unlimited power, Barth believed that all our comfort and all our defiance depends on our understanding anew that God is the "wholly Other"— namely the one who has limited himself. God bound himself to man, and specifically to sinful man. God did so by taking upon himself the legitimate no spoken to man in his wrongness in order to speak the even louder yes to this very same man. God determines himself free for fellowship with this man and thereby determines man to fellowship with him and with all whom he loves. He does this so that, in such fellowship, we may have and confirm our own mature freedom. From that point on, theology became more and more for Barth "theoanthropology."[6] That is, it became the doctrine of God and humanity and, therefore, a doctrine that looks to the *cooperation* of the *free* God and the *free human* person.

To describe this doctrine more precisely, and according to the Old Testament, Barth refers to it as the doctrine of Immanuel, that is, "God with us." God establishes his covenant, first of all and decisively, with the people of Israel, whom he chose for this purpose. But again, he enters into this covenant with a people who have not turned to him; he turns to them. But by turning to them, the extent to which they have turned away from him is exposed. For Barth, sin is turning away from God. Therefore, the more serious sin, Barth says, is not that found among the children of this world; rather, it is the sin of those who know themselves to be God's children. But even that sin that is uncovered among them, God covers and overcomes all the more by his gracious righteousness through the reconciliation of the cross.

This reconciliation is so radical that not only Jews but now even Gentiles have access to it. In 2 Corinthians 5, Paul speaks about matters that were basic for Barth: in Jesus Christ God has reconciled *the world* to himself. God not only wants it. He *has* done it by an act that nothing can supersede. He has reconciled to himself not only believers, not only Christians, but the "world," whether the world is aware of it or not, whether it acknowledges or denies it. Indeed, he breaks through our preoccupation with ourselves and with "our loved ones." God's act of reconciliation does not make the church unnecessary. Rather, it gives the church her purpose. According to Barth, the church exists, first of all, because she perceives in her midst that which is not yet perceived outside of her midst.

Barth loved to describe the church by the term *circus*, the Latin derivation of the word *church*, which literally means "vicinity" or "surrounding." He referred to the Latin translation of Mark 3:34, which says that Jesus called those who were gathered around him his brothers and sisters. They hear him (see 4:9). They perceive him. And if the fellowship of those who perceive him is the church, then it should become visible in this way: Christians must be those who from the very start, from their *baptism* on, perceive Christ. For Barth, it became obvious that true Christian baptism, just like the baptism of Jesus, is not an infant baptism but a mature baptism, that is, a baptism in which the one who is baptized says yes to the fact that God says yes to him. According to Barth, so long as the church does not perceive Christ, it cannot clearly see to its second reason for being.

The church's second reason for being is so that *all* her members may be *sent out* to people in their surrounding area. Each gathering together for the worship of God represents, for Christians, a pause to catch their breath in order to be sent back out again to their fellow humans. Therefore, the church is to celebrate communion each Sunday so that members may receive provisions for the journey on which the congregation has been sent. Being sent out does not mean that all members must do the same thing. But all have to do one thing: all must be witnesses of Jesus Christ and of his help and reconciliation. This idea then is not like the one developed during the Middle Ages when priests were sent out to the people or to church people; rather, the idea is that all members of the congregation are sent out as messengers of God to their neighbors, both strangers and friends alike.

After World War II, during countless long nights and demanding days, Barth continued to write one volume of the *Church Dogmatics* after another. As he did so, the clash between the Eastern and Western blocs weighed heavily on his mind.

The 1950s were times filled with hysteria. The name of the American senator, Joseph McCarthy, epitomized the battle in the West against those who did not keep to a strict anticommunist course, which meant, for the most part, a spoon-feeding of freethinking in the West. West German politics were also aligned to this course, thereby rubbing off on the Protestant churches in Europe. Former Nazis were now able to prove that they "had been right all along." These politics were also connected to the thesis that Swiss circles had quietly embraced in 1941: Hitler was really waging a war against the Soviet Union, not Europe.

Even in 1917, Barth had learned from Leonhard Ragaz to keep his distance from Russian Communism. But now he had more respect for Russia, realizing that it was primarily Russia that had won the victory over Hitler's Germany. Nevertheless, he repeated the words of Immanuel Kant to European youth gathered in Hungary during spring of 1948, "Have the courage to think for yourself!"[7] And during another lecture where he explained the importance of the Christian congregation, "the Church must be and must remain a Christian fellowship and live for its own concerns even in the midst of political changes."[8] This was the main tone of the position Barth now took.

Barth developed his thesis in the *Church Dogmatics* from the perspective of the Christian church. National Socialism had presented the church with the great temptation of conformity, but Communism had not. Yet because Barth said so, Emil Brunner now attacked him, saying that he was making himself the spokesman of those who were embracing "a truly diabolical system of injustice and inhumanity"[9] Barth answered that it certainly was not "the duty of the Church to give theological backing to what every citizen can, with much shaking of his head, read in his daily paper."[10] Shortly after this, a senior civil servant, Feldmann of Bern, attacked him sharply, saying that Barth "was showing a rather emphatically benevolent neutrality regarding Communism."[11] Barth's response that an agreement might be possible on common ground was not heard, and he remained silent to further accusations, even though he was attacked as if he were an enemy of the state in 238 different newspaper articles. He still believed that if churches in the East and West would only take seriously the task of being the *church of Jesus Christ*, they would become a *bridge* to overcome the dangerous conflict between East and West, which had heightened due to the atom bomb.

After World War II, Barth participated much more intensely in ecumenical efforts than in political activities. In 1948, the World Council of Churches asked him to deliver the keynote lecture for their first meeting in Amsterdam. Remarkably, he took the given theme of the conference, "The Disorder of the World and God's Plan of Salvation," and reversed it. He began by talking about God's plan of salvation and then spoke about the world's chaos. This was a typical pattern of his thinking. He thought by beginning as he did, the disorder of the world would become truly visible, and the other problems that the conference planned to address, problems such as the distribution of wealth, property, and capital, would not be forgotten. At the same time, he believed that only by beginning with God's plan of salvation would the church think properly of itself and not dare to do what only God alone is doing. "We are not the ones who transform this evil world into a good one. God has not abdicated his dominion to us. . . . That we should be his witnesses, the disciples and servants of Jesus, in the midst of the political and social disorder of the world is all that is demanded of us."[12] But as he prepared for the second meeting of the World Council of Churches in 1954 in Evanston, Illinois, he again tried to make very clear that the church is to be an active witness. The church serves as an active witness to a great hope because it "already now knows to recognize the coming King in his hungry, thirsty, alien, naked, and imprisoned brothers."[13]

Then a window to the Roman Catholic Church opened up for him when some of its theologians began to publish sensible books on his theology, such as Hans Urs von Balthasar's *Karl Barth: Darstellung und Deutung seiner Theologie* (1951)[14] and Hans Küng's *Rechtfertigung: Die Lehre Karl Barths und eine katholische Besinnung* (1957).[15]

Before and after the Second Vatican Council, a warmer climate and a lively relationship emerged between Barth and the Roman Catholic Church. The highlight came in 1966 when he was invited to Rome for conversations with Pope

Paul VI and leading Roman Catholic theologians. He wrote in one of his books that he dedicated to the Pope: "In common service to the one Lord, this book is dedicated to Bishop Paul VI, the most humble servant of God, by his separated brother Karl Barth." As a result, toward the end of his life, Barth wanted to write an "ecumenical theology." According to his plan it should not begin with the general concept of "religion," but rather with a particular Christian confession in order to come to terms with other confessional and church traditions, and then later extend to non-Christian religions.

Barth visited the United States for the first time in 1962 and was welcomed warmly as perhaps only Americans can do. There, he felt quite happy, giving several lectures under the title, "Introduction to Evangelical Theology." He also participated in discussions with leading American theologians. When someone asked what he would like to see changed in the United States, he answered: the prisons. For Barth, being in prison was almost like being in purgatory. He wanted to visit a prison because, in the past years, he had preached only in the penal institution of Basel. He said that he preached there because he was not so sure that the gospel would fit in the Basel Münster cathedral, but he was certain that the gospel belonged in prisons. As a result it was this American prison that clearly showed him the social problems of the country. At the end of his trip in Chicago, he said that what he wished for the United States was "freedom . . . for humanity." He understood that the Statue of Liberty was "a symbol of a true theology—not of liberality but of freedom, . . . the very freedom for which the Son (of God) has set us free and which, as a gift, is the only true human freedom there is."[16]

Barth became sick after this visit and suffered a stroke that temporarily took away his ability to speak. Just as a doctor was asking him questions, he pointed to his mouth and all of a sudden was able to speak. The first word that came out was the name "Zachariah," the father of John the Baptist who, according to Luke 1, had also lost his speech for a while. Barth became so healthy that he was able to lead seminars at the Second Council of the Vatican, on Calvin and, finally, on Schleiermacher.

The Tübingen theologian Joseph Ratzinger once held a superb lecture in one of Barth's seminars, and when he finished Barth said, "You have presented the Roman Catholic Church to us as such a magnificent church that we poor Protestants now feel rather small compared to it. But I ask you, I ask only humbly. . . . Is this church of yours not a clever escape from the Holy Spirit?" Karl Barth asked this question with great earnestness; for, according to his understanding, the goal of God's way is not the church but the new heaven and the new earth where justice reigns.

On the evening of his last day at the conference, he was writing a lecture and stopped in the middle of the following sentence: "God is not a God of the dead but of the living. They all live for him." He then called upon his friend of sixty years, Eduard Thurneysen, and talked with him. He concluded by saying, "Don't let your ears droop down, under any circumstance, for He reigns." When a dog is *alert*, its ears *stand up*. "He reigns" were also the final words of Johann Christoph Blumhardt. For Barth, God does not forsake the world. For God loves not only those we love but even those who are beyond the limit of our love; otherwise, he would neither love us nor our loved ones aright.

# Questions for Reflection

1. Does the kind of love God has, which, according to Barth, is always for others lead to a universal reconciliation or universal salvation? If so, is Barth still serious about God's justice and his judgment? Must God not condemn and reject wrongdoing? Does not such reconciliation provide an escape for evildoers who make the weak victims of their malice? And why then would we still need a Christian church or Christian ethics?

2. Does Barth's Christocentricity mean that he can no longer clearly state the difference between what God does as the creator and what new things he will do as the perfector? Does his Christocentricity mean that he is still able to respect the witness of the Jews? And, contrary to the questions above, does Barth assume that God will have mercy on people of other faiths? What about those who do not know Christ or reject him?

3. Barth apparently deviates from a wide consensus of Christian churches in his understanding of baptism as the beginning of Christian life and as affirmed by the one baptized, and he deviates in his understanding of the Lord's Supper as the strengthening of the congregation for its sending into the world. How are these sacraments understood in the Christian church? How does Barth's doctrine relate to this understanding? Does he destroy the concept of sacraments? What does the New Testament say to his doctrine?

# 4

# The *Church Dogmatics*: "To Think Is to Think After"

# THE FAITH THAT SEEKS UNDERSTANDING

W̶hen asked to respond to a newspaper article written by the atheist Max Bense, Barth entitled his response "To think is to think after." This sentence reduces his doctrine of knowledge to its least common denominator. Theology is basically thinking that cannot begin with itself. It follows that which goes before it and is given. Christian theology is entirely dependent on that which goes before it and is given. It cannot reason, prove, nor produce itself. It can only begin with itself, come from itself, and follow itself. With this we begin to understand this fundamental statement in Barth's doctrine of knowledge: What matters in theology is always and again "to begin at the beginning." This means that the beginning of our knowledge of God is "not a beginning which *we* can make *with Him*. It can be only the beginning which *He* has made *with us*" (II/1, 213 = 190). The one whose theology does not begin with God will never arrive at God.

But what is meant exactly by "the given" (*die Vorgabe*) from which theology lives? Barth begins by saying, first of all, that which is given is the church and her witness of God in word and deed. Yes, Christian theology exists only "because before it and apart from it, there is in the Church talk about God" (I/1, 2 = 4). Theology, therefore, is inevitably a churchly science. But the church speaks about God sometimes in a more or less good way and, yet at other times, in a "terribly confused and distorted" way.[1] This challenges theology to test the appropriateness of the church's speech about God. But theology has to test the church's proclamation by something else that is given that makes it possible for the church to speak about God—Holy Scripture. The church is only truly the church when she is bound to Holy Scripture. Whether she is properly bound to Scripture is left to theology to find out. The church herself has to read the Bible and pay attention to specific passages. Above all, she has to practice thinking and living according to the Bible's thought form (*Denkform*) (I/2, 918f. = 821f.). The Bible's thought form refers to the Bible's way of pointing beyond itself or, as Barth says, giving witness. Barth describes what the biblical witnesses proclaim, the given by which they speak about God, with the formula: *Deus dixit*, "God has spoken" (I/1, 114ff. = 111ff.). And since Holy Scripture is formed by the testimonies of these witnesses, theology can only carry out its task within the church when it aligns itself to the Bible and allows itself to be formed by it. Theology does this on the basis of the same presupposition by which the church's proclamation lives. It begins on the basis that God has spoken within the witness of Scripture and in *such a way* that this same God also speaks today. Therefore, theology not only has to test the church's past proclamation but also help new proclamation to take place. This is a brief summary of Barth's doctrine of the threefold form of the Word of God.

Among these three givens of Christian theology, the most decisive is the event in which "God has spoken." This is not about a presupposition human beings *make*. This given is about a pure *gift*. It consists of God allowing himself to be presupposed by humanity, yet in such a way that this given never changes into a presupposition humanity can make. "Revelation remains revelation and does not become a revealed state" (I/2, 131 = 118). God is also hidden in his revelation, which is "a gate which can be opened only from within"[2] and remains hidden insofar as this gate cannot be opened "from the outside." With respect to its decisive presupposition, theology stands with empty hands before this door. This is so because only God opens this gate and he does so by speaking to humanity. Holy Scripture, the church, and, therefore, theology are only able to speak about God because God has spoken and speaks. We ourselves cannot make God speak. And we do not *have to* because God already has spoken and continues to do so. It is precisely for this reason that *God* is known only by *making himself known*.

That God speaks to humanity is not and will never be a presupposition that falls into our hands. Barth calls this event, as already pointed out, the Word of God or revelation. Barth did not introduce the specific concept of "revelation" to theology. During his early liberal days, he participated in the rather fashionable use of this word and could, for instance, speak about Goethe as a revelation of God.[3] But he later was disturbed by the use of this concept when German theologians in 1914 saw "the war, in all seriousness, as a revelation of God."[4] Indeed, in 1926 he referred to this concept as a "magic key" in the hands of neo-Protestant theologians by which "man becomes wholly master even of the self-revealing God."[5]

He therefore placed this concept under critical scrutiny. In doing so, he fully acknowledged the legitimacy of modern questions concerning knowledge of God. But just as the reformation excluded any earning of God's grace through human works, he now excluded access to God through any human capacity of knowledge.[6] Revelation does not merely mean that man begins to know God. The basic claim is "God is known *by* God and God is known *only* by God" (II/1, 200f. = 179, rev.). Barth was dealing here with the question of whether our knowledge of God is based merely on a human monologue, and thus an illusion, or whether what we "*allegedly*" say about God is "*really* about Him" (I/1, 169 = 163). Theology is necessarily defenseless with respect to the question of proving this. Theology itself cannot provide this presupposition, which is so decisive for its speaking. Only God himself can prove that he *is*, and is not an *illusion*. Only God can keep "man from dreaming if he supposes that a second entity standing over against him" is that basis and justification for his talk about God.[7] There is certainly a great deal of such dreaming. And this is what Barth's criticism of religion is about. What is meant here is certainly not a barbaric "contesting of the true and the good and the beautiful which a closer inspection will reveal in almost all religions" (I/2, 327 = 300). Barth, in contrast to Dietrich Bonhoeffer, also does not think that one can, even as an atheist, simply set religion aside. He is also not concerned about criticizing particular religions. It is about a criticism of religion *as such*, and not even a criticism performed by Christians. Indeed, it is a criticism performed, first of all, on them by God alone and by God himself in his revelation. Here is where religion is exposed. Contrary to what it pretends to be, religion is "a complete and thoroughgoing fiction, which has not only little but no relation to God. It is an anti-God who . . . can be known as such, as a fiction, only as the truth does come to the believer" (331 = 303, rev.). Religion is "the attempted replacement of the divine work by a human manufacture. The divine reality offered and manifested to us in revelation is replaced by a concept of God arbitrarily and willfully evolved by man" (329 = 302).

Only the light of revelation reveals the person with whom God is dealing, namely, that this person is detached from God, a godless person. Yet it is precisely this fact that human beings deny by acting religiously and, thereby, giving the impression that they have been dealing with a God for a long time. Revelation "does not reach us," therefore, "in a neutral condition," nor even on the way to such. It reaches us as religious people who, as such, deny our godlessness. It reaches us "in the attempt to know God from our standpoint. It does not reach us therefore in the activity which corresponds to it," but rather in our "resistance to it" (329 = 301–302). But we will realize this critical judgment only when "all that we think we know about the nature and appearance of religion" does not serve as a standard for God's revelation, but rather when "we have to interpret the Christian religion and all other religions by what we are told by God's revelation" (309 = 284). Only this will disclose that by satisfying his religious need, a person is merely turning to his own "reflection" (345 = 316). Although he believes he is dealing with "Another" in religion, he is only dealing with himself. But the protest against this lies in the Old Testament's prohibition of images, basically saying that God can only come to humanity through God. If a person, himself, reaches for God, he actually only reaches himself. "Because [religion] is a grasping, religion is the contradiction of revelation" (330 = 302–303).

Is Barth contradicting himself when he nevertheless acknowledges "*true* religion" (356 = 325)? At any rate, it means that religion does not necessarily have to be equated with unbelief. By itself it is probably nothing else. But the fact that it can also be something different has its basis, according to Barth, in the incarnation of the Word of God. For, according to John 1:9, he who now appears is the "true light, which enlightens *everyone*, was coming into the world" (emphasis added).[8] Barth sees it like this: when the Word of God "came to . . . his own" (John 1:11), it does not force something strange on man. Yes, everyone stands "necessarily, by order and structure in relation to [God]," so that as Augustine says, "our hearts are restless until they rest in Him."[9] Barth says this reference to man's God-relatedness is not necessarily but factually overcome by sin. Sin does not destroy this longing of the human heart that is restless until it rests in him. But sin distorts it in such a way that revelation is not to be seen within this longing but, rather, this longing is to be seen in the light of revelation.

But we come back to Barth's statement that only God himself can prove that he is and is not an illusion. Is this thought not an excuse that avoids Ludwig Feuerbach's charge that faith in God is an illusion? Barth took this charge seriously.[10] But with regard to it he said: the statement that only God himself can prove that he is, is a *consequence*. It follows the confession that God *has* already proven it. "God *has* spoken." We are confronted here with a basic structure of thought in Barth's theology. Kornelius Heiko Miskotte put it into this formula: "Reality has precedence . . . over possibility."[11] The reverse is typical of modern thinking. Descartes, for example, begins with the self-assured reality of his own self in order then, from this perspective, to point to God as a conceivable possibility. He then claims that that which is possible must also be real. But by doing so, he only proved that God was a thought the self could think. Barth turns this kind of thinking on its head, or, rather, on its feet. We can always and only begin with the fact that God has *really* turned to us. This reality is more certain than our own life. Only later can we seek to understand how this is possible and conceivable.

Related to this principle for Barth is another important principle, namely, the precedence of the concrete over the general. He often pronounced it in two Latin warnings: *Deus non est in genere* ("God does not exist in general") and *Latet periculum in generalibus* ("Danger lurks in generalities"). With regard to our knowledge of God, this principle refers to the task of taking our concepts and their meaning in the general sense and allowing them to be continually corrected by the concrete reality of God's turning to us. These two principles are connected to a further principle, namely, that true knowledge of God takes place in what Barth called a "wholesome circle": I could not have found God without seeking him again and again. This sentence corresponds to Barth's claim that God's revelation also includes his veiling. But if God's revelation takes place even in his veiling, we can also say that I cannot seek God without having already found him. Otherwise, I would not know who I was looking for.

How does one get into this circle? God *brings* one into it. God does so by freeing and calling one to faith in God. With Luther, Barth says that man "in his own reason and strength can neither believe in him nor come to him" (IV/1, 833 =

745). Yet Barth emphasizes at the same time that faith, as a human action, cannot in itself and as such save man. "Faith does not realize anything new. It does not invent anything. It simply finds that which is already *there* for the believer and also for the unbeliever. It is simply man's active decision for it, his acceptance of it, his active participation in it" (828 = 742). "Faith stands or falls with its object" (828 = 742). Even for Barth this important word, "object" (*Gegenstand*) is not easy to understand. It does not mean the same as the word "thing." An object normally refers to something that a human being (the "subject") can own and master. But for Barth this is precisely what the word "object" does *not* mean. In German, the term translated as *object* literally means "that which *stands in the way* of anything that seeks to master it." If God is the object of faith, this means that God is not in the hands of the believer but that faith is entirely dependent on God. It has its center, its life, and its truth in him. Barth describes it like this: God in his revelation certainly "comes into the field of man's consideration and conception in exactly the same way that objects do." But "knowledge of this object can in no case and in no sense mean that we have this object at our disposal." We have "all other objects . . . because we first of all consciously have ourselves." However, "Only because God posits Himself as the object, is man posited as the knower of God" (II/1, 13, 21–22 = 13, 21–22). Therefore, "Christ remains the object of the Christian faith, even though He lives in Christians and they in Him. Its gravity and its liberating power depend upon the fact that the believer is not alone by himself, not even in a supreme ecstasy of union with his Lord" (I/2, 131 = 118).

Barth could have thus also said that by God's positing himself as the object, the human subject is posited as the one who *believes*. Clearly for Barth, as already for Calvin, faith and knowledge are most intimately related. This does not mean that faith is merely a matter of the mind. It is that, but it also is a matter of the heart. Yet the word "knowledge" guards against attributing a creative power within human beings in relation to this work of God. The main point is that man perceives God's truth through faith, but it is not made real by him. It is in this light that Barth describes faith by three "activities": acknowledgment, recognition, and confession (*Anerkennen, Erkennen, Bekennen*) (IV/1, 847 = 758).

I will now give special emphasis to the second concept, recognition. Christian faith is not a blind acceptance of rules but is already in itself an apprehending recognition of God's Word. Such recognition is nothing strange to faith but something already present in it, if it is a faith that seeks to understand what it believes. This is not only a task for specialists. The spread of Bibles, catechisms, and confessions within the church shows that all Christians are entrusted with this task. They are all theologians too. Yet this does not exclude the fact that some are specifically called to be professional theologians.

Their task has just been named. It is about "seeking to understand what they believe." This sentence is a translation of the Latin formula *Fides quaerens intellectum*, which Barth discovered in Anselm of Canterbury, a theologian of the Middle Ages. In 1931, Barth published a book with this title. He later confessed that he had written this book in particular "with the greatest love." The title indicates the path of knowledge taken in the theology of his *Church Dogmatics*. The formula substantively says the same thing as the subtitle of this chapter: "To think is to think after." Theology is thinking after that which we believe. Or, to say it with Anselm's formula, theology is the task of seeking to understand that which faith believes. This does not mean that the "I" of the theologian is the material of this science. Nor does it mean that some church doctrine is necessarily to be held as true. What it means is to understand *what* the church of Christ believes, namely, the Word of God out of which the church was born and which creates faith in her, that is, the Word of God as attested in Holy Scripture by which God makes himself known.

*Knowledge*, therefore, is in accord with faith because that which establishes it is *truth*. Man does not already know by himself what truth is so that by this standard he can then find out whether God's Word is true. But it is in the hearing of God's Word that one is confronted with the truth that awakens him to faith and to knowledge and to an understanding of that which is believed. As faith precedes knowledge, it signals to us that the knowledge we gain here will deal with the one true object. This is *the* object that cannot be controlled, but also that which theological knowledge presupposes, is founded upon, and deals with. Basically, the knowledge and understanding of this truth, therefore, can only ask "*to what extent* is reality as the Christian believes it to be?"[12] Barth takes this one step further. We cannot deduce the truth of God from *our* knowledge of his truth just as we cannot deduce God's existence from our existence. It is much rather the other way around. Because God is the truth "therefore he exists."[13] For this reason God reveals himself as the One who is the *truth and* who *is* in truth. But as we *recognize* this truth, our *existence* is then taken into account as well. And by faith in God we recognize not only who *God* is but also who we are as *humans*.

## Questions for Reflection

1. Is theology necessarily a churchly science? Can it be bound to the church if it wants to be a science? What is the difference between Holy Scripture and church proclamation? And what is the difference between Holy Scripture and the Word of God or revelation? If Barth sees a difference with regard to the latter, can we agree with it? If so, why? If not, why not?

2. According to Barth, is God hidden within his revelation? Are not the terms "revealed" and "hidden" mutually exclusive? Does this mean that God reveals himself only partially? Or what else could be the meaning of putting together these otherwise contradictory terms?

3. Is what Barth says about "religion" actually clear? He says, first of all, that "the true and the good and the beautiful" is found in religion and such may not be despised. Second, he says that religion is "a complete and thoroughgoing" fiction. Third, he says there is also "true religion." Does Barth not contradict himself in these statements? Or is there a way to explain how these statements might be correct in their proper context?

4. Barth's doctrine of theological knowledge is summarized by Anselm's phrase: "faith seeking and asking for knowledge or understanding." There are other teachings to consider in this regard, for example, Paul Tillich's teaching that theology speaks in the correlation of existential questions and theological answers or Wolfhart Pannenberg's view that faith can only believe insofar as it has gained theological insights. Compare these different approaches and try to take a position on them.

# THE FREEDOM OF THE TRIUNE GOD

Barth's exposition of the doctrine of the triune God, the Trinity, is among the "most important ones of the entire work" of his *Church Dogmatics*.[1] He treats it in a rather unusual way by dealing with it at the very beginning of his enormous work. And yet he does not then simply set it aside as if it were a topic already dealt with. Rather, he returns to this beginning point again and again, looking at it ever anew. In his doctrine of preaching, he was strictly opposed to sermons that "waste one's time with introductions rather than coming to the main point."[2] In a similar way, he began his *Dogmatics* with its "main theme" by dealing, first of all, with the doctrine of the Trinity. It is this doctrine, according to Barth, that "basically distinguishes the Christian doctrine of God as Christian . . . in contrast to all other possible doctrines of God or concepts of revelation" (I/1, 318 = 301). Why does this doctrine have such high significance above all others? And why in presenting the whole of Christian doctrine does it need to be at the beginning? In order to answer these questions, we must simply ask how Barth understands the triune God.

Let us look for an answer by considering the statement that Barth describes as the root of the doctrine of the Trinity. The statement is, incidentally, deliberately modeled after the frequently repeated pronouncement of God in the Old Testament: "I am the Lord." Barth puts it like this: "God reveals Himself as the Lord" (I/1, 324 = 307). In order to understand this phrase, we have to be clear about its terms. He writes, "If we inquire how, according to His revelation in Jesus Christ, God's lordship differs in its divinity from other types of rule, then we must answer that it is lordship in freedom." In contrast to other sovereignties, freedom here is the privilege of divine sovereignty. But freedom here does not merely mean the absence of limits that is claimed against others in one's own favor. Freedom here means, above all, "to be grounded in one's own being, to be determined and moved by oneself" (II/1, 339 = 301). Because God is free in this sense and not by disassociation from others, he is therefore also free to have fellowship with and be faithful to his partners in such fellowship (341 = 303). But he does so without ceasing to be free in such a relationship. "God's self-unveiling remains an act of sovereign divine freedom" (I/1, 339 = 321).

That God reveals himself as Lord, Barth explains with a statement he elaborates in three parts (I/1, 332–352 = 315–333): "Revelation in the Bible means the self-unveiling, imparted to men, of the God who by nature cannot be unveiled to men" (332f. = 315f.). First, God does that which human beings can never do: "He makes Himself present, known and significant to them as God" (333 = 315). He comes so close to them that they can call upon him personally, by name. God does not *have* to do so, as if he would be poorer in himself if he did not. God is rich in himself. But God *can* do so. And he does in order that *human beings* might be made rich by it. By doing so, a "differentiation" within God himself emerges. This makes him at the same time both a God inwardly concealed and outwardly revealed. God is free to make such a decision. This shows that God is not only in the highest but is, at the same time, a God of the lowest depths of misery. The language of the church puts it like this: God is revealed in the "Son" (338 = 320).

Second, the sentence cited above means that God certainly gives himself in giving his son, but in doing so God does not give himself away. It is in *this* sense that Barth says that God in his revealed essence is not unveiled. His revelation of himself is not the kind of mystery that is unveiled to us and then no longer remains a mystery. If God were such a mystery, his revelation would mean that human beings could have power over God and, in his name, oppress others. But no! "God is always a *mystery*" (339 = 321). God always goes his own way with us precisely by being "God with us." Revelation does not mean "a loss of His mystery" (342 = 324). The one to whom it is revealed is thus continually dependent on God. As God reveals himself to us, he is free to encounter us again in a completely different way—and even then remains the same in himself. As this irrevocable mystery takes place in the self-unveiling of God, he reveals himself precisely as the "Father" of the "Son."

Third, the sentence cited above refers to the fact that the self-unveiling of the veiled God is *granted* to *us*. This presupposes the unity of the self-unveiling and veiled God, the unity of God the Son and God the Father. It is in this unity that God turns to us and opens himself to us. To us? Yes, Barth says, but this happens in such a way that God "becomes God to specific men" (350 = 331). It does not happen by our applying some general idea to ourselves and to our circumstances. Rather, it happens in such a way that people are affected by it only *concretely*, and nothing is known about it apart from this concreteness. God reveals himself to them in such a way that they in return become open to him. Otherwise, they would never be open to him. But it happens in following and responding to the "message" God gives them. Just as a veiling of God takes place on Good Friday and an unveiling at Easter, so too is this the message at Pentecost. God's revelation of himself as the Lord means that he communicates with humans. And this means that "God reveals Himself as the *Spirit* . . . as the Spirit of the Father and the Son, and therefore the same one God, but the same one God in this way too" (351 = 332).

Barth summarizes this entire train of thought: "revelation must indeed be understood as the root or ground of the doctrine of the Trinity." This means that talk about revelation does not yet constitute a developed doctrine of the Trinity. But even more important, without God's self-revelation in history, there would be no doctrine of the Trinity. It is the foundation for it. Yet the doctrine of the Trinity is not directly found in Scripture, despite several liturgical formulas such as 2 Corinthians 13:13. It is a construction of the church of the fourth century and was acknowledged by the church as an important exegesis of the revelation of God in Christ. This doctrine says that the God named in Scripture is the Father, Son, and Holy Spirit, not three gods but one single God whose tri-unity is essential to his being. Barth was reluctant to call these three "persons" because in modern times the word *person* is understood as "individual." Thus, three individuals by themselves could not express the unity of the triune God (IV/1, 224 = 204–205). Barth preferred the phrase: one God in three "modes of being." The expression "mode of being" (*Seinsweisen*) indicates that God is not only the triune One in his revelation. But he is the triune One because he is so "beforehand in Himself" (I/1, 411, 442, 490 = 390, 420, 467). The one God, as Father, Son, and Holy Spirit, has a specific function in these three distinct ways of being: the Father is God in his sovereignty, the Son is God in his humility, and the Spirit is God in the connection of the Father and Son. "But this one God is God three times in *different* ways" (I/1, 380 = 360).

Christian theology does not, therefore, represent a deviation from "monotheism." According to Barth, it quite clearly teaches there is only *one* God, according to the witness of Deuteronomy 6:4 and Mark 12:29-31 (I/2, 419–421 = 381–383). But all of this has to do with the unity and uniqueness of the triune God. Therefore, Barth resists the reduction of the unity of God to a monad. "This neutral Godhead, this pure and empty Godhead, and its claim to be true divinity, is the illusion of an abstract 'monotheism' which usually fools men most successfully at the high-water mark of the development of heathen religions and mythologies and philosophies. The true and living God is the One whose Godhead consists . . . precisely *in these three modes of being* the One God, the Eternal, the Almighty, the Holy, the Merciful, the One who loves in His freedom and is free in His love" (IV/1, 222 = 203).

If monotheism is reduced to this abstract sense, there are two significant consequences, both of which result in Christianity's self-negation. The first is the emergence of a basic works' righteousness. For if God is understood as monotheistic in this sense, the question arises as to how then God can be mediated to human beings. Such a monotheistic God is not able to achieve such mediation.

Barth remarks that such a god is "the prisoner of its simplicity." And he adds, "The god of all synergistic systems is always the absolute, the general, the digit 1, the concept" (III/3, 157 = 139). In the same context, he says that this god is an "*idol*." Here he already touches on the second consequence of such a reduction of monotheism. As one tries to come into contact with God by his own actions, he deals only with a product of his own making, with a picture he himself creates of God, all the while violating the second commandment: "You shall not make yourself any graven image." Man-made religion will be nothing else "but a reflection of what the man is and has" (I/2, 345 = 316). Instead of God, he will worship an anti-God. But he will not admit it because he will carry out this act religiously. "But it can be known as such, as a fiction, only as the truth does come to him" (331 = 303).

Barth intensifies his critique of this understanding of religion and places it in direct contrast with revelation that comes to humanity from God: "If man tries to grasp at truth of himself, he tries to grasp at it *a priori*. But in that case he does not do what he has to do when the truth comes to him. He does not believe. If he did, he would *listen*; but in religion he talks. If he did, he would accept a gift; but in religion he takes something for himself. If he did, he would let God Himself intercede for God; but in religion he ventures to grasp at God. Because it is a grasping, religion is the contradiction of revelation, the concentrated expression of human unbelief" (I/2, 330 = 302–303).

In further elaborating his doctrine of the Trinity, Barth critically distinguishes between his position and, on the one hand, the effort to substitute God for an idol and, on the other, the problem of works' righteousness. The Trinity, we learn here, means that God is *one*. In his nature, in his "person," God alone is one. In calling God Father, Son, and Holy Spirit, according to biblical language, the Christian faith does not deny but, rather, teaches the equality of essence of these three, the "identity of substance" of this very God (I/1, 370 = 351). What we are dealing with "precisely in the Church doctrine of the Trinity as such . . . is Christian Monotheism" (371 = 351). Are the anti-Trinitarians, who have shown up at times in the church, not rightly concerned about the unity of God? Yet it must be said against them that they "are denying either the revelation of God or the unity of God" (371 = 352). Either way, because God's intervention into time is foreign to them, they commit idolatry with a Jesus whom they conceive to be a mere man or "half God." As long as the anti-Trinitarians do not recognize one God in the Trinity of Father, Son, and Holy Spirit, they will not turn from their error.

The Trinity means on the other hand "that God is the one God in threefold repetition" (369 = 350). This repetition is thus based in God, and he is God in this repetition. God is not in need of a second and then a third beside himself in order to be God. But "in Himself these limits of what we otherwise regard as unity are already set aside" (374 = 354). There is no loneliness in him. He is not dependent on his creatures to have a counterpart. Rather, it is his creatures that need him as a counterpart in order to live. He himself turns to them and gives them what they need essentially to live.

At this point, we can certainly understand why the doctrine of the Trinity, according to Barth, is of such absolute importance for Christian theology. It basically says that which is both simple and fundamental at the same time: we are united with God because God—and God alone, but God indeed—cares about this union. All true God-relatedness rests entirely upon an act of free grace in which God himself turns to the human creature while the human creature remains entirely dependent on God. At the same time, God takes care that this very human creature turns on his part to God. Barth recognized that the ancient church's knowledge of the doctrine of the Trinity and the Reformation's knowledge of humanity's salvation belonged together, inseparably. He even said that the ancient church doctrine, correctly understood, is the "natural presupposition" of the Reformation's doctrine of salvation (440 = 419). It is the presupposition of the doctrine of God's act of grace and the work of his Spirit, of his comfort and claim. As the triune One, he is on the scene from the beginning, and in his time he enters the depth of our being and in the end will shine as the eternal light.

In sum, "who is the Lord and therefore also the God" who is called "Yahweh in the Old Testament and Kyrios in the New" (405 = 384)? The New Testament attributes true divinity to Someone other than Jesus, namely, to "Father of the Lord Jesus Christ" (407 = 386). But if this Christ reveals God "then irrespective of His creaturehood He Himself has to be God" (427 = 406), and truly God, without reservation: "To confess Him as the revelation of His Father is to confess Him as essentially equal in deity with this Father of His" (427 = 406). And so also is the Holy Spirit "God Himself, to the extent that He can not only come to man but also be in man, and thus open up man and make him capable and ready for Himself, and thus achieve His revelation in him" (473 = 450). Barth sought in this way to promulgate what he called "Yahweh-Kyrios. . . . The doctrine of the Trinity is not and does not seek to be anything but an explanatory confirmation of this name" (368 = 348).

## Questions for Reflection

1. Does the doctrine of the Trinity really have such high significance as Barth claims? How do we understand Christ and the Holy Spirit if the doctrine of the Trinity is denied? Is there really such a close connection between the ancient dogma of the Trinity and the Reformation's confession regarding humanity's salvation by grace alone? Or is this confession of the Reformation still valid if the doctrine of the Trinity is denied?

2. Barth sees the root of the doctrine of the Trinity in the sentence: "God reveals Himself as the Lord." What is the difference between God's free sovereignty and

an authoritarian power? Or is there really no difference? And if the answer is yes, what is the most convincing argument?

3. Barth sees the root of the doctrine of the Trinity not only in the New Testament but also in the Old Testament. What kind of arguments can be made to support such a claim? Formulate possible objections to them and discuss them.

CHAPTER 4.3

# THE COVENANT OF GRACE
# MADE WITH ISRAEL AND
# FULFILLED IN JESUS CHRIST

Barth loved the motto: *Non sermoni res, sed rei sermo subjectus est.* "The word serves the content, not the content the word" (I/1, 374 = 354). Thus the meaning of the concept of covenant must be "read out" of "*the* covenant-history" to which "the entire Bible testifies" rather than the other way around, namely, that a preconceived notion of the covenant is "imported into" the Bible (IV/1, 59 = 56, rev.). A "covenant of grace" as a general concept may seem foolish. But, in *this* covenant, it is the main point, and as such it is not merely a covenant to be taken "*cum grano salis*" (with a grain of salt), as Barth said in earlier years.[1] Now he insists that the covenant is *originally* and *decisively* about a covenant of grace.

Barth was not only a dogmatician but also an exegete. In contrast to other dogmatic works, his is filled with passages of detailed exegesis of Holy Scripture, both of the Old and New Testaments. In order to give an example, we will look at how he laid the foundation for his doctrine of reconciliation in God's covenant on the grounds of biblical testimony. He did so by listening closely to Jeremiah 31:31-34 (IV/1, 32–35 = 32–34). He rejects interpretations that eliminate the "covenant with Israel" in favor of the "new covenant." There should be no question about its cessation because "the elements are exactly the same as in that covenant with Abraham, Moses and Joshua which is normative for the Old Testament as a whole. The formula 'I will be your God and you shall be my people' . . . is emphatically enough endorsed" (32 = 32). Barth insists that the new covenant allows no talk of *two* covenants of God or a replacement of the covenant with Israel with another. There is only the *one* covenant of God. "What God will do in accordance with this prophecy will be a revelation and confirmation of what he had always willed and indeed done in the covenant with Israel" (34 = 34). What then is the meaning of the "new," "eternal" covenant that Jeremiah 32:40 refers to? According to Barth, the "complete change" (33 = 34) envisaged by this covenant "does not concern the 'substance' of the covenant but its 'economy' (Calvin!)" (32 = 32, rev.). It is about the change of *the* form of the covenant "in which it is revealed and active in the events of the Old Testament this side the last days" (32 = 32). It is about an alteration of this "form in accordance with the completely changed conditions . . . so radically, that it will no longer be recognizable in that form and to that extent a new covenant will actually have been concluded" (32 = 32). It is about a "change of structure" of the covenant with Israel of which it is "capable" and "which it will undergo in the last days." It is about its "replacement . . . only in the positive sense," "that it is *upheld*, that is, lifted up to its true level, that it is given its proper form, and that far from being destroyed it is well maintained and confirmed" (32 = 32, rev.). Precisely *because* the newness of this new covenant consists in *such* a positive replacement, it does not consist of a replacement in the negative sense. The covenant with Israel is neither dissolvable nor is the new "covenant" really a *covenant* anymore.

Jeremiah 31:31-34 announces a threefold "*intensive* amplification" of the covenant concept. First of all, this covenant will no longer be "like the covenant which I made with their fathers . . . which they broke" (v. 32, RSV). God will write his law "upon their hearts" so that he shall be their God and they shall be his people (v. 33, RSV). As Barth understands it, because of the breaking of the covenant on the part of the people, the new covenant "which in its earlier form is open on man's side will in its new form be *closed*." It will be "*mutually*" kept "not because men will be better but because God will . . . turn them to Himself. To His faithfulness—he Himself will see to it—there will then correspond the complementary faithfulness of His people" (32–33 = 32–33). Second, in the new covenant *all* will know God. This means putting an end to "the fatal controversy between God and man and it also means the ending of the corresponding necessity . . . for that human antithesis or opposition between wise and foolish, prophets and people, teachers and scholars." Paul describes the end of this antithesis (2 Cor 3:6-18) with his doctrine of the old and the new covenant: the one of the prescriptive letter, the other of the liberating Spirit, which leads to obedience (33 = 33). Third, the new covenant is new in that God "will forgive them their sin." This *eliminates* the broken covenant and leads to the inward gift of the *Spirit* and to the knowledge that the new covenant does not remove but completes the old one. This is what forgiveness is about. "God Himself negates— the unfaithfulness of Israel, but not the faithfulness of God Himself . . . to his people" (34 = 34).

Two things follow, according to Barth. First, because the new covenant does not abolish the covenant with Israel in the negative sense, we can say that even now the covenant with Israel already lives by what the new covenant reveals. The new covenant is the *revelation* of the foundation on which the covenant with Israel, in a hidden way, already stands. Moreover, in the covenant with Israel, "for all the antithesis between the faithfulness of God and unfaithfulness of man, and the divine judgments that follow this antithesis . . . do we not find something of the forgiveness of the guilt and the gracious forgetting of the sin of His people . . . which in fact obviously answer to the deepest being of the covenant? And on this basis were there not always in this people new . . . hearts, and the Spirit and freedom, and even a simple and genuine keeping of the commandments?" (34 = 34). Second, since the new covenant abolishes the covenant with Israel in this positive sense and adds an "intensive *amplification*" to it, the "most exclusive part" of this covenant is also to be understood as inclusive. In Jeremiah's prophecy, the Old Testament looks "beyond the past and present to a form of the relationship between God and Israel in which the covenant broken by Israel will again be set up, that the Israelite, for whom ultimately God has nothing but forgiveness, but does have it actually and effectively, must now take his place directly alongside his Gentile fellows, and that if at all he can hope for the grace and salvation of God only on this presupposition" (35 = 34).

Let us look now at Barth's systematic reflections on these exegetical insights. This covenant is the one sealed by God with Israel and made definitive in Jesus Christ. Indeed, it is the covenant of grace in which people of the "gentiles" are now also included. That which is called covenant here is stated in the formula by which God pronounced himself the God of his people and humankind to be his people: "I will walk among you, and will be your God, and you shall be my people" (Lev 26:12; II/1, 542 = 482). According to Barth, all this certainly has to do with a two-sided covenant. In his covenant of grace there is then "no God but the God of the covenant" and as a result "no man but the man of the covenant" (IV/1, 40, 45 = 39, 43).

But this must be stated more precisely. Barth repeats here what he has already explained in detail in the doctrine of election. The covenant does not come about by God first making decisions about others. God, first of all, elects and determines *himself* to be "the companion" of man and thereby elects and determines him as "His own companion" (IV/1, 53 = 50–51, rev.). First and decisively, his partner does not decide to belong to this covenant. The partner can only subsequently confirm that God has determined him to be his partner. The partner then must not and may not remain passive. He must *gratefully* observe the covenant made by God and *bear witness* to it by his actions. That is all he has to do. This is so because the human partner does not deserve that God enters into a covenant with him. The covenant is called a covenant of grace because it lives and continues to exist only by the fact that God in his grace still turns precisely to this partner. This is about a covenant between two *unequal* partners. It has to do with God's gracious character and not abstractly with the difference between God and human beings. They are unequal because "God is the merciful Lord and because man is the covenant-partner who shares but also needs this divine mercy" (III/1, 177 = 158). In such mercy God has allied himself with *Israel*.

"The gods of the ancient world surrounding Israel also had their own peoples and these people had their gods," but it was "in a reciprocal relationship of solidarity and control" (IV/2, 871 = 768). Wherever the relationship between God and humanity is thought of in *such* a way, there is no covenant of grace. Rather, such thinking opposes the covenant of grace and leads to "natural theology," which is religion without grace (112 = 101). This kind of religion must then deny that *only* Israel is first chosen to be a part of the covenant of grace just as natural theology denies this choice. And yet, "If ever Israel takes up the attitude to God that its relationship with Him is one of *do ut des* [I give so that you give], . . . then it is *unfaithful* to its own election as His peculiar people and to its own electing of God. It has already fallen away to the worship of false gods and the transgression of all His commandments" (IV/1, 26 = 25). The covenant made with Israel is of a *different* kind. Its two-sidedness is determined by its one-sided foundation through God. For the covenant "is not that Israel has chosen Him, but He Israel" (IV/2, 871 = 768). "This covenant does not discover Israel already existing as such but it creates Israel" (I/2, 88 = 80–81; IV/1, 184f. = 169f., according to Deut 32:6). Because Israel has been chosen thus by God, the church, which has been called from among the Gentiles, can and must only marvel that she too has been called.

Barth called the part of his dogmatics that deals with this the "heart" of the Christian "message" (IV/1, 1 = 3). Originally, he intended to call this part the doctrine of the *covenant*. But he decided to call it the doctrine of *reconciliation*. Either way, the concepts belong together. Both do not say the same thing, but they refer inseparably to each other. Man with whom God makes his covenant is not fit to be God's partner because he is a sinner. God can only enter into a covenant with man by forgiving and overcoming his sin. God then carries out this covenant in the form of reconciliation. Barth basically declares, "Reconciliation . . . is the fulfillment of the covenant between God and man" (IV/1, 22, 71 = 22, 67). But how is this understood more precisely?

It should first be said that Christ's reconciliation is God's *reaction* to sin (37 = 36). In fulfilling his covenant, God cannot unite with man without reacting to the fact that he is a sinner in rebellion against God. Reacting? Barth knows well that a mere reaction would only lead to being pulled into the undertow of that which one reacts against (I/2, 709 = 633). If reconciliation were *only* a reaction to sin, it could be continually "put into question" by sin, even "made impossible" (IV/1, 71 = 67). God's *covenant* is not this kind of reaction. It is the *action* of the God who anticipates all sin. In relation to him, every sin comes too late. Only as God actually confronts the problem of sin does it take on the form of a reaction against sin. But because the reaction as such takes place "along the line of that action determined from the very first in the will of God and already initiated" (37=36), it is not, therefore, in a powerless position with regard to what it reacts against. For it is "even in this particular form the accomplishment of God's covenant will" (37 = 36). It is in reconciliation that the covenant *truly* reaches its goal and is not left pending. Since the covenant is a covenant of *grace* from the beginning, it can be fulfilled by *reconciliation*.

Barth's understanding of the covenant has an unusual emphasis at this point when he says that God involves himself with humans *despite* sin. But the reason he says this is because, if it were otherwise, God's relationship to human beings would be dependent upon sin. Sin would either be immortalized or God would have nothing to do with humans apart from sin. As God's reconciling reaction to sin takes place in the act of his covenant will, it cannot thus be pulled into the undertow of sin. For God, this can only mean allying himself with human beings notwithstanding their sin (73 = 68). According to Barth, the reconciliation that takes place in the fulfillment of God's covenant has the character of an effective *protest* (71 = 67). Barth even speaks (and here he uses the concept in a different way than usual) of the character of *judgment*. Because it takes place as a reaction to sin in God's covenant action, his judgment is the fulfillment of God's faithfulness as he rejects Israel's unfaithfulness (34 = 34). But his gracious faithfulness has this strict form because it is not the "weak remission" (666 = 597) of a God who is powerless with respect to sin. The heart of reconciliation is "the *overcoming* of sin" (278 = 253). God's judgment and his grace are not in tension with each other, but both are in tension with respect to *sin*. God can only reconcile the sinner with himself by not reconciling himself with that which is wrong with the sinner. God's judgments over biblical Israel are then actually only signs because Israel is not the one who has to suffer God's judgment (II/1, 445 = 395–396). These judgments are to be understood only within the framework of God's covenant with Israel and not in terms of Israel's rejection from it (438 = 390). He who is judged by God "can be sure that God *receives* him in this judgment" (II/2, 820 = 734).

Yet Barth also defends a counter thought that needs to be considered in order to properly understand the specific relationship of covenant and reconciliation. Reconciliation certainly takes place *within* the covenant. But also reconciliation is so essential that the covenant would risk falling "in the void" (IV/1, 72 = 68) were it not fulfilled by *reconciliation*. And this, according to Barth, refers, first of all, to *that* Israel with whom God originally allied himself. That reconciliation took place *within* the covenant means "with divine necessity" (184 = 168) that the Word became flesh, yet "not simply any 'flesh,' any man humbled and suffering. It became Jewish flesh. The church's whole doctrine of the incarnation and the atonement becomes abstract and valueless and meaningless to the extent that this comes to be regarded as something accidental and incidental" (181f. = 166). From the beginning of time, the covenant—a fellowship of God and his people—has been threatened with dissolution by the breaking of it from the human side (71 = 67). Reconciliation is the overcoming of this break *and* also the overcoming of the threatening dissolution of the fellowship between God and his own.

This overcoming happens through the Son of God who "took our place." All the practices of those who had broken the covenant are excluded through him. Barth understood 2 Corinthians 5:19 to mean that "He who knew no sin took our place and status . . . accepted solidarity with us sinners, in so doing He made our place and status as sinners quite impossible" (80 = 75). In *this* way God's grace is his judgment and his judgment his grace. This happens neither by God being gracious to some and not to others, nor by him merely condemning sin but allowing the sinner to go free, or by pronouncing himself guilty and pronouncing the sinner free. The very heart of reconciliation is the "overcoming" of sin and the sinner (278 = 253). In this light the Old Testament judgments are understood as mere signs of the final judgment that has now taken place for the sinner and his sin. At the same time, it is here confirmed that whenever God's judgments took place in the Old Testament they occurred in the framework of the covenant of grace. They are "the great commentary on *the* fulfillment of *that* covenant" (26 = 26). Whereas in the Old Testament the covenant is presented as a series of *many* conclusions of the covenant, with the Son of God, who took our place, the covenant became *definite* because it was "filled" with reconciliation (24 = 24).

Christ's reconciliation means then that the covenant with Israel is not *replaced* by another covenant. It means its *fulfillment*. Thank God the covenant is *not* invalidated because its fulfillment consists of a reconciliation that shows God's covenant of grace to be a "grace for lost sinners" (73 = 69). Non-Christian Israel's rejection of the fulfillment of the covenant in Christ cannot annul this covenant but only confirm it. The church, therefore, has to confess the eternal election of Israel (II/2, 225 = 204). Because the covenant with Israel is fulfilled in this way, this covenant now *opens up* for *other* sinners besides Israel and becomes a covenant between God and *humanity*. These are such bad sinners that they do not even know how bad they are. But there is no other covenant made with the nations. "There can be no question of anything but their inclusion in the one covenant" (I/2, 115 = 105). But those who have become members of this covenant can only be sure of its validity for themselves as "grace for lost sinners" as they confess its validity, first of all, for all Israel. Otherwise, Christianity would risk getting such assurance by substituting self-affirmations, which often occurs when one separates oneself from others. Reconciliation as the basis for the permanent election of Israel includes the reconciliation of the *world* with God, which includes all people "whether they are aware of it or not" (IV/1, 270 = 245). It does matter whether they are aware of it. They should be aware of it. They will be made aware of it. But they can only be made *aware* of its validity. They cannot *make it valid*.

Here, according to Barth, we must take a closer look at a certain *twofold form* of the covenant of grace. It is introduced to us in the relationship between the Old and the New Testament. The church has to distinguish between the two testaments, but not by seeing them in opposition but, rather, in their unity. The Old Testament is the book that speaks in expectation of the covenant's fulfillment. The New Testament is the book that speaks in recollection of its fulfillment (I/2,

50 = 45). Barth immediately speaks about this in a more differentiated way. The Old Testament confesses the coming fulfillment while such expectations are being fulfilled. And the New Testament remembers this fulfillment as Christ's church witnesses to that for which she waits. The church, therefore, has to read *both* testaments, and this is a double movement: "what came before was only with a view to what comes *after*" and "what comes after only in view of what came *before*" (IV/3, 76f. = 70f., rev.). The church reads Scripture in light of the fulfillment of the covenant through the reconciliation that took place in Jesus Christ. But, in this light, the church is not released from this back-and-forth movement. For the fulfillment of the covenant is not about a new one; rather, "it is the one covenant . . . which is only now fulfilled in *this* form . . . because it is only now immediately and directly conformable to its basis, content and goal as the reality of the Messiah Jesus latent in what came before, in the history of Israel and its prophecy" (IV/3, 75f. = 69f.). In such a reading, the church puts the factual question to the synagogue: "Can the closed Canon of witness to expected revelation be read with meaning apart from the counter-canon of revelation that happened?" (I/2, 111 = 101). The church has to be open to the insights of Jewish exegetes who, as "'pure' students of the Old Testament," point objectively to the unity of the Scripture (87 = 80). The church also has to be clear about the fact that just as the fulfillment of the covenant does not remove the covenant with Israel, so the church has a wrong understanding of the *New Testament* if she separates it from the Old Testament or if she reads the Old Testament merely as a "historical adumbration" of the New Testament (I/2, 86f. = 79f.). And the reverse is also the case: just as the covenant with Israel without its fulfillment ends up "in a void," so the church does not take the Old Testament seriously if she reads it apart from its fulfillment.

The twofold form of the covenant of grace, however, does not merely mean for Barth this difference between the biblical testaments. He speaks about a further difference, namely, the difference between Israel, who was called first (Jews who believe in Christ are also part of this), and those who were called from among the Gentiles. However, the difference lies not in a distinction in their dependence upon the forgiveness completed in Jesus Christ. *All* are in need of forgiveness. But Barth says this within the context of his statement that, in the reconciliation, Christ reveals "this *covenant with Israel* is made and avails for the whole race." For this reconciliation reveals "that the meaning and power of the covenant with Israel for the whole race is that it is a covenant of free and therefore effective *grace*" (IV/1, 35 = 35). Herein lies the difference between the Israel who was elected first and those called from among the Gentiles. Members of the first chosen people of Israel are the first witnesses of the covenant of grace in both the Old and the New Testament. This covenant of grace has been made with Israel. But because of Christ's reconciliation, it is now truly filled with grace and, therefore, also opened up for the Gentiles. Barth liked to say, according to Isaiah 42:6 and 49:6, that they are "a mediator of the covenant among the nations" (II/2, 126 = 117; III/1, 133 = 120; IV/1, 30 = 29; IV/2, 178 = 160; IV/3, 561 = 488; IV/4, 221

= 201). It is justified then that "Israelites are attesting all this to us (in the Scripture)—and since, as we were told the witnesses of revelation belong to the revelation themselves, it is necessarily Israelites. . . . If we want it otherwise, we will have to strike out not only the Old but all the New Testament as well, replacing them by something else which is no longer a witness of divine revelation" (I/2, 566 = 510). And where the church in "Christian anti-Semitism" seriously understands herself as the "successor of Israel" (II/2, 319f. = 290f.), her witness becomes indeed "superfluous" (257, 318 = 234, 289, rev.).

# Questions for Reflection

1. If God's covenant with his people is a covenant of grace from the outset, what else does reconciliation have to offer beyond it? And why would this covenant without reconciliation end up "in a void"? How can this be a true covenant if God is the one who not only makes himself man's partner but also determines man to be his partner?

2. According to 2 Corinthians 5:19, God has reconciled the world to himself. Barth's understanding here is that Christ took our place and thereby made it impossible for us to remain as we were. Is this a proper exegesis of the meaning of reconciliation?

3. If Scripture speaks of an old and a new covenant, why does Barth then explain that there is only one covenant of God? If it is a covenant in two forms, is it still only one covenant of God? How do Christians read the Old Testament? Are they any different than the "pure students of the Old Testament" among the Jews?

4. In the ecumenical dialogue of the churches, Judaism is officially counted among other religions. Barth, on the contrary, sees Jews and Christians together in the one covenant of God fulfilled by reconciliation. Discuss different perspectives on this issue. And do so in light of Luke 15:11-32.

# THE EXTERNAL BASIS OF THE COVENANT AND THE INTERNAL BASIS OF CREATION

With his thesis of *one* covenant of grace fulfilled in Christ, did Barth simply evade the problem of a "covenant of nature," which in his early days he sought to honor? Or in his rejection of a "covenant of nature" did he encourage a kind of forgetfulness of nature and leave an entire realm isolated from divine interest yet exposed to unlimited human access?[1] My thesis is that Barth did not evade the problem. Rather, he criticized the modern treatment of it. And, from his understanding of the covenant of grace (II/2), he opened up new insights in his doctrine of creation (III/1). He did so in his analysis of the Roman Catholic doctrine of "nature and grace" and Emil Brunner's work, *Nature and Grace* (1934). Substantively, Barth was concerned here with the rejection of so-called natural theology. But his rejection of natural theology does not have to do with a rejection of the doctrine of creation but rather with a correct understanding of it. Natural theology not only recognizes God apart from Christ, but it acknowledges a different being than God. According to Barth, it makes God so much into "an element of our own . . . existence" (II/1, 157 = 141) that he becomes accessible to us in any way we please.

Barth explains in blunt terms that this understanding of God is the description of an "idol," which can never "lead . . . to knowledge of the real God" (II/2, 94 = 86). But the dangerous thing is that God's revelation can also be interpreted by such natural theology. Barth, thus, asks Emil Brunner, "For of what use would be the purest theology based on grace and revelation in the way in which natural theology usually deals with its alleged data derived from reason, nature and history, that is, as if one had them pocketed?"[2] The true God rather is known only when he *makes* himself known to us. His revelation is pure grace. Barth appropriates here the Reformation understanding that emphasizes, against Pelagianism, that God's act of relating to us *is* a matter of grace, but also, against semi-Pelagianism, that God's grace *remains* grace forever.[3] Correspondingly, this needs to be said with respect to knowledge of God. If God's revelation is a matter of grace, then this gift by which God makes himself known cannot become simply a given. God *in* his revelation is a *mystery* not at our disposal. We are not then able to know God in such a way that "we turn our backs on God's word," thinking that we have already understood it and now merely have to ask how to tell others about it (I/1, 249 = 236).

If the doctrine of creation is not to be presented in terms of natural theology, then how should it be presented? Barth responds to this question in an amazing way by his detailed exegesis of Genesis 1 and 2 in his *Church Dogmatics* III/1. And it is precisely here that he uses a variety of biblical commentaries, and especially the commentary of the Jewish theologian Benno Jacobs. Barth does not understand the biblical reports about the creation as historical (*historische*) reports, but as sagas. For him, a saga is "an intuitive and poetic picture of a pre-historic reality of history which is enacted once and for all within the confines of time and space" (III/1, 88 = 81). Genesis 1 and 2 offer two different sagas, and Barth summarizes their message in two sentences: for Genesis 1, "Creation is the *external* . . . basis of the covenant" (III/1, 107 = 97), and for Genesis 2, "The covenant is the *internal* basis of creation" (261 = 231). His doctrine of creation reflects these two sentences.

The first statement *distinguishes* between creation and covenant. This is not to deny that it is the same God acting here and there. But we must first know *who* this God is that created heaven and earth, and we must first recognize *for what reason* God created everything in order to know, specifically, that *he* is its creator. By disregarding his covenant, we will recognize a *different* God in creation. But the following sentence speaks against such a move: "There is only *one* revelation" (IV/1, 47 = 45). This sentence explains, once again, how Christians understand monotheism. It does not mean, abstractly, that God is *one*, rather it means, concretely, that God is *no other* than this one who turns to and unites himself with his creature and has revealed himself as such. And the creature's reason for being can only be understood in the history of God's covenant with his creatures. It shows that creaturely existence is the external basis for this unity, a basis established by God himself. For in his covenant with his creatures, he makes them *his presupposition*. The "external" presupposition of God's love for them is their existence. They do not have this of themselves. God creates this presupposition. Creation is God's work of "making possible the history of His covenant with man" (III/1, 44

= 42). This excludes the claim of a covenant of nature that is different than the covenant of grace. Just as the law is the form of the gospel (see 4.5), so creation is only recognized as a reality in its fulfillment through the covenant determined by the covenant-making God.

The second statement about the covenant as the internal basis of creation *relates* the concepts of covenant and creation to each other. It contradicts what Barth called the "dual system of book-keeping" (III/1, 476 = 414). He is speaking here about the effort to divide between a special sphere filled by God on the one hand and a godless and graceless secular autonomy on the other. The sentence says that since the covenant is the internal basis of creation, the *same* God who is at work in creation has chosen to be in covenant with his creature. By presupposing the existence of the creature, God *is* his creature's *precedent*. From the beginning, he is the God of the covenant who has chosen his creature to be his companion. From the beginning, he refuses to be neutral and have an existence that can be manipulated by our arbitrariness. For the *love* of God for his creature *precedes* its existence. How wonderful! The creature cannot enter into existence without being loved (III/2, 173f. – 145f.). "The fact that the covenant is the goal of creation is not something which is added later to the reality of the creature, as though the history of creation might equally have been succeeded by any other history. It already characterizes creation itself and as such, and therefore the being and existence of the creature" (III/1, 262 = 231).

For Barth, both of these statements are to be spoken in the knowledge of faith that God has made his covenant with Israel and has fulfilled it in Jesus Christ. Seeing both statements together makes clear that the *distinction* between creation and covenant is not about the assertion of a world having been emptied of God and his grace. The distinction alerts us to the fact that with creation we are dealing with the God of the covenant and not a *different* God who would disregard the history of the covenant or invite us to do so. But creation should neither be understood as a self-determined reality into which the work of the covenanting God must fit. The opposite is the case. Creation corresponds to the covenant of God. Creation, therefore, is neither the covenant itself nor a neutral background for it. Creation corresponds to the covenant but not of itself. It corresponds to it by God calling and bringing it into correspondence with his covenant. This is the reason that Barth delineates between an "analogia entis" (a relationship of correspondence based on shared being) and an "analogia revelationis" (a relationship of correspondence established by revelation) (III/3, 59 = 51). For a long time this was the decisive basis for Barth's criticism of the papacy. Roman Catholic theology formulated the former Latin phrase to say that we can infer things about the Creator from the creatures because the creatures share a "commonality of being" that is ordered by nature towards God and related to him. Barth formulated the latter Latin phrase and said that only because God speaks to us in his "revelation" does he make us his children. God thereby places us in relation to him. From this perspective, we are to understand what it means to be created by this same God.

The reality of creation corresponds to the covenant between God and humans in this twofold truth: "God is not alone" and "man is not alone" (III/1, 26f. = 25–26). The first statement says that God grants existence to something distinct from himself. He does not *have to* do so in order not to be alone. He is eternally not alone. But if God does not will to be alone together with this created other, it follows that this other is truly distinct from him. The fact that God is not alone is the basis of the independent *reality* of the created world. This is asserted against pantheism (III/3, 98 = 86), which teaches that God and the world are one. But it also contradicts the understanding of the world as a mere appearance in "my" consciousness (III/1, 27 = 26). The second statement says that humans need God in order to be human. This is not at all about "absolute dependence."[4] Man *owes* his existence to God who *grants* it to him. Therefore, man's existence is identical with the fact that God has not forsaken him. This makes human existence a *good* existence. Even limitations as a creature are part of having been created good. Because God created all things good, evil is not, according to Barth, God's creation. Again, creaturely existence is not a result of the Fall.[5] The existence of the creature is rather praise—whether quiet or loud—for this gracious God (IV/3, 796 = 695–696). In this sense, creation corresponds to the covenant God made with it. And God continually orders creation in relation to the history of the covenant (III/3, 43 = 38). This insight has three consequences.

First, because creation *is* coordinated with the covenant, it only needs to be *preserved* in it. This preservation is a history as well but a history of preservation (III/3, 37–38). Barth, therefore, rejects the neo-Protestant theory of "an ongoing creation" (*creatio continua*). Such a view subjects creation to limitless growth. Or, more precisely, it makes *the human creature* into a titanic (co)creator and, as such, unworthy of God. For "the Creator-God of the Bible is not a world-principle developing in an infinite series of productions. His freedom is demonstrated in the fact that His creative activity has a *limit* appointed by Himself, and His love in the fact that He is *content* with His creature as a definite and limited object, and has addressed Himself only but totally to it as such" (6 = 7). Therefore, the creature is only a creature "within its limits" and this signifies nothing evil. "The creature will only stumble at a supposed imperfection or obscure fate . . . when it does not admit or accept these limits" (96f. = 86f.). Its limits are not evil. The human creature imagines that the more it would seek to remove its limits, the better and more perfect and independent from God it would be. Yet the human creature's limitation is not evil because God wants to be *faithful* to his creature and thereby vouch for its existence within its limits. Just as God in his *love* to his creature affirms its existence, so also in his *faithfulness* he affirms that his creature *remains* within its limits. The God of the covenant, "the God of Israel," is also "the King of the world" (200 = 176). And as such he takes care to *preserve* his creature.

Second, creation demonstrates the appropriateness of the covenant, according to Barth, by the constant *relationships* within which the human creature lives in spite of sin. A typical way of expressing this is that humanity "in its basic form is fellow-humanity." This is also true when the human creature lives in contradiction to it. "He merely proves that he is contradicting himself, not that he can divest himself of this basic form of humanity. He has no choice to be fellow-human or something else" (III/2, 344 = 285–286). "The man who is not the fellow of others is no real man at all" (IV/2, 474 = 421). By this he contradicts *himself*. "But provision is made that man should not break loose from this human factor" (III/2, 344 = 285). Insofar as he cannot break loose from it, his humanity is a *parable* that reflects the covenant between God and humanity, and a *hope* that the covenant will find fulfillment in Jesus Christ. Because God does not let go of the fellow-human, God commands that the fellow-human not let go of him.

Third, that the creation is appropriate to the covenant means, according to Barth, that it is *irrevocably* good. The human creature certainly sins against its goodness. But he cannot destroy it because he cannot destroy the covenant to which the goodness corresponds. Evil is not denied, though. It is so powerful that it is too powerful for us. We are particularly weak against it when it tempts us to deal with it ourselves (III/3, 413 = 358). In the fulfillment of the covenant, *God* made the controversy with evil his own cause (89 = 79). And as this covenant is the inner basis of creation, it now counts. Just as the creature does not exist without God's affirmation, so evil does not exist without God's negation. Creation is *therefore* irrevocably good. This statement makes sense to the extent that one recognizes that the "truth of the covenant is already the secret of creation, that the secret of the covenant includes the benefit of creation." God's covenant with his creature in Israel's history, his becoming human in Jesus Christ from the "seed of Abraham, . . . shows the benefit enjoyed by the creature as such because bestowed in the act of creation" (III/1, 380f. = 332f.). The creation that God made good is not then rejected in the promised new creation. What is rejected is the perversion that broke into the created world by sin. In the new creation, a perverted humanity in a perverted world is not made better, but is actually made into an *old* humanity in an *old* world. This emphasizes the fact that the existence of the creature — within its limits—was not perverse but *good*, and it *is* and *remains* good. But the new creation accomplishes this because it is "more" than creation. It is *new* because it is not a consequence of that which was before, but of that which substantively precedes all things (IV/1, 52f. = 50f.; IV/3, 259 = 226–227). It is new because of the radiance of God's glory that shall never again be darkened by any contradiction (II/1, 729 = 648). And as the new creation has already intervened in the world in the fulfillment of the covenant through Jesus Christ, it is now known to the world as the promise that is being wonderfully fulfilled through God (2 Cor 5:17, see IV/1, 343 = 311; IV/3, 346 = 300). Because God has reconciled the world to himself, he has given it such a future: "the *perfecting* of its creation by the new creation of its form in peace with God and therefore in and with itself" (IV/3, 363 = 315). The gift of creation and the coming of the new creation are both then under the sign of the one covenant of grace.

# Questions for Reflection

1. In conversations between Christians and those of other faiths, it might appear that finding common ground can be best achieved through the theme of creation, whereas the theme of the "revelation of God in Christ" provides little basis for agreement. Yet Barth wants to understand creation in light of the revelation in Christ. Is his approach not more problematic than helpful? In his view of creation, how is it possible to have a conversation with scientists? Assuming that Barth recognized this question, why is it that he nevertheless took this kind of approach with regard to this topic?

2. The thesis of an "ongoing creation" is common among theologians, and it seems to agree with scientific claims. What exactly is meant by this thesis? Are you convinced by it? If so, what are your reasons? Why does Barth say no to it? What are his reasons?

3. This chapter includes some foreign words that you should be able to understand and discuss. What does Pelagianism and semi-Pelegianism mean? Why did the reformers distinguish themselves from it? Is Barth right in applying this distinction to the theme of the knowledge of God? What does *analogia entis* mean? In what sense does Roman Catholic theology use this category and what interest do they have in doing so? Why is Barth against it? What does his contrasting formula, *analogia revelationis*, mean?

CHAPTER 4.5

# THE CONTENT OF THE COVENANT-LAW AND THE FORM OF THE COVENANT PROMISE

The question has already been asked and now we return to it again: to what extent is this divinely and *one-sidedly* founded and sustained covenant of unequal partners still a *two-sided* covenant? For this, according to Barth, is "the aim and meaning of the covenant willed by God" (II/2, 134 = 125). The fact that God in his solidarity with humanity makes the human person to be his covenant partner does not mean that humans are merely "the object of the divine activity" (III/3, 74 = 64). The covenant of grace aims at the human person as his own subject who is "set on his own feet" (IV/3, 1082 = 942, rev.). In his covenant God wants to deal "as Partner with partner" (III/4, 747 = 649), with one who "in all his non-deity . . . is a real partner" (III/1, 207 = 184, rev.). In God's self-election for the covenant with his creature, God determined to give "autonomy, not that these gifts should be possessed outside Him, let alone against Him, but for Him" in order to confirm his sovereign love. This love does not want to rule "over puppets." It wants "to triumph in faithful servants . . . in their own free decision." This free decision, which in its freedom is in accord with the will of God, Barth calls the true "autonomy of the creature" (II/2, 194f. = 177f.).

According to Barth, this has especially to do with the purpose of God's *law*. God's covenant grace and his covenant law belong together as both are to be seen together in this way: "His promise by which He binds and pledges Himself to man and His command by which he pledges and binds man to Himself" (IV/1, 56 = 53). This commandment demands that a person *be the one* God has made him to be, namely, his partner. To be, then, a partner is given to him and, at the same time, *thereby* commanded of him. God brings *himself* in relation to man and God brings man into correspondence to himself. It only remains for man to confirm this by the act of gratitude (43 = 42). Thus "He constitutes Himself the Lord of the covenant. . . . He gives it its content and determines its order. He maintains it. He directs it to its goal. He governs it in every respect. . . . The covenant-member is the one whom He ordains. It is what He wills that takes place within the covenant" (II/2, 8 = 9). Because God himself becomes our partner and also makes us to be his partner, he now "expects and demands" from us, his covenant partner, responsibility. Responsibility means living in such a way that answers God's call, a call in which God takes up responsibility for humanity. Thus God takes such responsibility to be the purpose of human existence. For "grace does not will only to be received. . . . It wills also to reign. . . . There is no grace without the lordship and claim of grace" (II/2, 10f. =11f.).

Such ethics are not only grounded differently than other ethics but also differ in character. This is seen in the *one* thesis that Barth considered the "basic substance" of his dogmatics (IV/3, 427 = 370): "The one Word of God is both Gospel *and* Law. . . . In its content, it is Gospel; in its form and fashion it is Law. It is first Gospel and then Law. It is Gospel which . . . encloses the Law" (II/2, 567 = 511). The objection that both are mixed when the gospel does not have its own non-legal form,[1] fails to see in Barth's explanation a clear *precedence* of the *gospel* before the law. The gospel proclaims what God alone does in uniting us to himself and uniting us to him. The concept of "form" appears only where it pertains to the understanding of the *law*.[2] The term *form* tells us that the *law* of God is not to be separated from the content of the gospel that "fulfills" it. It is fulfilled, first of all, by the action of a gracious God. God first bound himself to humanity (II/2, 821 = 735) and claimed *himself* for humanity (567 = 511–512). Therefore, his law does not meet us as an abstract decree. It meets us first of all as the law that God himself obeys. At the same time, what is good and what is evil has been so thoroughly decided that we no longer have to make that decision. And this makes those whom God's law addresses accepted as his very own from the beginning because he himself has taken responsibility for them.

Second, the law is fulfilled by him who became human and who agreed to reject our sin for us. He thereby fulfilled the commandment of God "in our place." The law counts because God is the doer of the law in the One who became human. And God commands us only because "He Himself . . . has fulfilled what He orders" (627 = 565). The law of the gracious God meets us then as the law twice-*fulfilled*. This is what Paul calls in Romans 8:2 "the law of the Spirit of life." The law is *thus* the "form" that the preceding gospel sets up for itself and apart from which the gospel does not exist. In it no stranger puts a claim upon us. But it is God's law that puts a claim upon those who *belong* to *him* through Jesus Christ who has taken "our place." As God unites himself to us and us to himself, as he takes up responsibility for us and proves himself to be responsible before God in "our place," it is *right* that his gospel has *this* form by which it determines our action to be in conformity with his. "How can God will and create this covenant, or man exist in this covenant, or God be gracious to man, without this determination of man?" (II/2, 639 = 575). In his law God determines that we live as his covenant partners a life that is in conformity to his action as the covenanting God. And because as the *form* of the gospel his law is always and already *fulfilled* law, it conforms itself to the gospel. It is *gracious* law. According to its content, "the command of God . . . will always set us free along a definite line. It will not compel man, but burst open the door of compulsion under which he has been living. . . . It will not appeal to his fear but to his courage. It will instill courage and not fear in him." In this way it is the *easy* yoke, "the assumption of which is in every sense our quickening and refreshing." The person not refreshed by God's command "is not the obedient man but the man who disobeys God" (651 = 586).

Wherever the law is separated from its gospel fulfillment, it becomes the *mere* form of a demand that must be *fulfilled* by *man*. He thus "misuses" the law,[3] no matter whether it is achievable. He then does not obey God but someone else. "A law apart from the gospel hopelessly enmires us to the service of both God and mammon."[4] This is where sin offers its "master stroke."[5] The problem with breaking the covenant is not the transgression of "laws" as if the problem could be solved if the laws were kept. The problem is in understanding God's command as that which must first of all be fulfilled by us, as if it were an unfulfilled law without grace. But wherever we perceive the law as already fulfilled, we perceive it as a divine claim, that our action "should become and be always that of those who accept God's action as right" (II/2, 638 = 575). "And when Israel does *keep* the commands of its God, . . . it will necessarily appreciate that the knowledge and experience that He is its salvation and righteousness, and the blessing in which it stands, are God's *free* grace" (IV/1, 26 = 25). By keeping the commands, humanity will not *establish* a two-sidedness of the grace covenant. Humanity will only *confess* in it a two-sidedness established by God and in so doing will become a witness to God and his covenant (III/4, 80 = 73).

With Calvin, Barth calls our consent to live according to God's free covenant grace "free obedience." In Barth's view a forced obedience is just as little obedience as a disobedient freedom is actually freedom (see II/1, 38f. = 36f.; III/4, 12 = 13). It sounds like a contradiction when Barth says that God "compulsorily places [us] into the freedom of obedience" (IV/1, 34 = 33). But he is obviously speaking here about the presupposition of free obedience created by God *alone*. But what is at issue here is the *freedom* exercised by "independently active and free subjects" (IV/3, 383 = 332). The existence of those "who have lost their independence by the illusion of independence" is the existence in *sin* (IV/1, 517 = 465, rev.). God's grace sets us free from such an existence and "addresses [each of us] as an adult" (IV/4, 25 = 22–23, rev.). But such freedom is *given* to us. We owe our freedom to our inclusion into the covenant of grace and to the fact that such freedom is carried out in accordance with the covenant. Our freedom, therefore, is autonomy within the conditions created by God. In these conditions, we choose *that* which God chose for himself and for us: existence within the covenant of God to which we belong by God's determination prior to our own self-determination (II/2, 192f. = 175f.). Human freedom then is obedience in that it *conforms* to the use that God makes of his own freedom.

*Prayer* is for Barth the characteristic act by which one participates as a member of the covenant. As the *unequal* partner of God, the human partner turns to God, petitioning him and responding to his mercy. But as God's partner, a person does so in his own maturity. Already in his doctrine of election, Barth says, "God's eternal will is the act of prayer . . . this act is the birth of a genuine human self-awareness, in which knowledge and action can and must be attempted" (II/2, 197 = 180). In all this, humans discover that God "is God in the fact that He lets man apply to Him in this way, and wills that this should be the case. Here, then, we stand before the innermost center of the covenant between God and man" (III/4, 102 = 93). The work of obedience first commanded of us is prayer (103 = 93). As we obey, we follow Jesus Christ who fulfilled the covenant, entering into it from the human side, by his free obedience. This is particularly exemplified in his prayer (II/2, 134f. = 125f.). Subsequent to his prayer, we are active covenant partners, and thus the basic form of the entire Christian ethos is actualized. Therefore, the common denominator of the ethics of reconciliation is "from the Christian standpoint we may describe as good and permitted and commanded . . . as a work of the freedom for which Jesus Christ has freed his own, and for which they are free in the power of his Holy Spirit . . . the human action . . . [that] takes place in the required responsibility of the children of God to their Father and therefore in the course of their calling upon him" (*Das christliche Leben*, 144.178 = 108).

# Questions for Reflection

1. After he was expelled from Germany during Hitler's reign, Barth nevertheless returned to Germany one last time in 1935. He did so in order to present a lecture on his new understanding of gospel and law. It was his clear word of farewell to Christians there. Can you imagine why communicating this understanding of law and gospel was especially important to him at this time?

2. Barth defends an unusual thought, namely, that freedom and obedience are not opposed to each other and cannot be divided from one another such that one could be free in certain areas yet must obey in others. Freedom and obedience belong together. Do we agree with this or do we have a different understanding of

freedom and obedience? What might Barth say to such different understandings of freedom and obedience?

3. Another surprising thought is that prayer, above all things, should be the first act of obedience demanded of us. Why should this be surprising? Are there any objections to this thought? Do you know of any arguments that might support this thought?

# THE EXPOSURE OF SIN IN LIGHT OF ITS OVERCOMING

I s it not obvious that sinners recognize themselves as sinners? In 1948, Barth wrote, "Six million Jews were murdered. . . . Horror and agony of every kind fell upon humanity. But all that has come and gone as a wind blows over the . . . flowers: they are bowed for a while, but when the wind stops, they raise themselves again. . . . In the words of the modern drama, 'Once again we got by.'" Yet all this did not expose "our lostness and condemnation in such a way that we can no longer escape it by ourselves."[1] From his context, Barth saw in his doctrine of sin a striking disconnect between grave deeds of injustice and serious awareness of it. But diminished awareness of injustice certainly does not diminish the vast injustice of the deeds. This has been the way ever since the Fall. In his doctrine of sin, Barth asks how does one come to the point where one beats one's breast and confesses, "I have sinned" (Luke 15:21).

It is apparently part of sin that the one who commits it does not admit it. The sinner has countless ideas how to cover up sin, to deny it, to reinterpret it, to minimize it, and to blame it on someone else. According to Barth, the most sinister aspect of sin is when the sinner takes the measure, the law to detect sin or "nothingness," as Barth says, into his own hands. "There are few heresies so pernicious as that of a God who faces nothingness more or less unaffected and unconcerned, and the parallel doctrine of *man* as one who must engage in independent conflict against it" (III/3, 415 = 360). Barth shows it is precisely this concept that is so widely spread within modern theology (IV/1, 413–427 = 374–387). In his judgment, the sinner makes a distinction between his better self and his bad deeds

(447 = 403–404). He certainly *has* sins but *is* not a sinner. He overestimates himself and underestimates his sin. "The moment man acknowledges that he is a sinner he is already comforted (because he has never really been discomfited)" (447 = 374). Barth says, however, that the sinner only truly knows about his sin when he finds himself in all his wrong deeds "in an inescapable way accused and in a definite way condemned." "This is what *thou* doest! This is what *thou* art!" (413 = 390).

How does one really know one's sin? The answer is "that *only* when we know Jesus Christ do we *really* know that man is the *man of sin*, and what sin is and what it *means* for man" (430 = 389). Sin becomes visible where Jesus Christ has borne it in our place, and he bore it as that which for God himself is "an intolerable menace of His whole work" (455 = 411, rev.). It is as intolerable for God as it is for us. But Christ offered himself in order to overcome that which is intolerable. And, according to Barth, we have to say it in this strict way: the overcoming of sin is the nonreconciliation of God with this intolerability. The reconciliation of the sinner with God in Christ is also God's serious and effective contradiction of the wrong by which the sinner contradicts God (II/2, 837 = 749). Reconciliation does not improve the "old man" of sin but in it God puts an end to him (IV/1, 432 = 391; IV/2, 549 = 485–486; II/2, 825 = 739). Reconciliation is an affirmation of man that at the same time confronts man the sinner with "a No in which there is no hidden Yes" (IV/1, 453 = 409). Whenever reconciliation is thought of apart from this No, it becomes reconciliation with the wrong. In this context one can understand Barth's often-misunderstood statement that sin is "no possibility except that of the absolute impossible" (IV/1, 454 = 410). This sentence says that the sinner is not merely doing something forbidden. This would mean that humans are free to break the law. According to Barth, the sinner does not have such freedom because there is no reason whatsoever to sin, no reason in God or in humanity, whom God created as good. Just as ethics deals with the law fulfilled by Christ, so the doctrine of sin deals with the confusion of the "old" self killed by Christ.

Yet doesn't Barth lead us in all this to see sin as "no longer relevant in actuality"?[2] Let us take a closer look. He emphasizes "the proof of man being a transgressor lies precisely in the fact that he continually is trying to deny this" (II/2, 829 = 742). Only where one knows oneself loved by God is one free to admit one's guilt. Forgiveness of sin is the opposite of repression of sin in that the latter leads to sin being pushed aside and unspoken yet still rumbling sinisterly about. Repression of sin is graceless existence. On the other hand, forgiven sin does not mean forgotten sin. "The statement that sin is forgiven does not mean that there is no longer sin in our self-knowledge. . . . We have not received forgiveness . . . if we do not acknowledge and confess our sin . . . if we do not maintain the responsibility which we owe to God for what we are and do . . ." (II/2, 845 = 756; IV/1, 666 = 597). Two things then lie behind the one whom God pardons: the previously unforgiven and unrecognized sin. And what lies before the one whom God pardons is the forgiven sin, the sin recognized in the light of forgiveness, which drives one to repentance. The pardoned sinner's thinking then is in accord with God's reconciling yes to the sinner and God's irreconcilable no to evil. The Bible, therefore, sees those who fall away "'almost exclusively within the sphere of the *community* . . .' *You* who are evil"![3] Of course, Barth noticed that some Christians were not aware of this at all, and he liked to allude to Luke 16:8: "the children of the world are sometimes wiser than the children of light." He takes into account that non-Christians sometimes see an analogy to evil within the troubles of life more clearly than Christians (IV/1, 397f. – 360f.). At any rate, wherever sin is not recognized, others are accused. Whoever recognizes it, knows that sin "does not exist except as his sin" (IV/1, 446f. = 403f.). And wherever it is not recognized only a general complaint is made: "We are all sinners." The one who recognizes it concretely will actively repent.

Although sin always appears in a particular form, according to Barth, it basically "always and everywhere" has three dimensions. They are "rebellion against God, enmity with one's neighbor and sin against oneself" (IV/1, 440 = 398). These three things are connected to each other in such a way that if a person transgresses in one area he at the same time transgresses in the other two. Wherever he is against God, he becomes a wolf to his neighbor.[4] And "if I am inhuman, I am also . . . godless" and self-destructive for "I cannot and will not be an I without a Thou" (IV/2, 498f. = 442f.). And if I am self-destructive, I will also become "deaf" to God and "useless for society" (IV/2, 520f. = 461f.). The sinner appears here as one who is alone in a dangerous way: "The solitary man is . . . the enemy of all" (IV/2, 474 = 421). But, at the same time, it needs to be seen and said that the lonely "are sick with isolation" (IV/2, 500 = 443).

Barth now connects this perspective on sin in an artful way with two further points, each of which having three aspects. First, sin is rebellion against him in whom God has humbled himself in becoming human; that is, it is *pride*. Second, sin is rebellion against the person whom God has exalted to be near him; that is, it is *sloth*. And sin is rebellion against the truth revealed to us about God and humanity; that is, it is a *lie*. But let us take a closer look at the further explanation of these sins. As he speaks about pride, Barth is not supporting a servile mentality. He used to say that there is a "pure Christian pride." Yet the sin of pride is rebellion against the God of the gospel, who places his sovereignty in solidarity with the humble. Man in evil pride puts himself in God's place, in the place of a false and inhuman god, and so he himself becomes inhuman. He now engages in the exploitative battle of competition and makes "war" to be the "father of all things" (IV/1, 501 = 451). War, "always the holy one," obviously has an ideological, indeed, a religious source. But man also transgresses against himself in pride. He becomes "a marionette pulled by wires in a group of men who all share the same illusion of independence" (IV/1, 517 = 465). But pride also relates to the sin of sloth.

Barth does not simply say that sloth is sin. He likes Franz Overbeck's suggestion that we should "consider erecting in a side-chapel a small altar to idleness" (III/4, 636 = 554), and he suspects that the modern celebration of work promoted by

Protestant ethics "is a symptom of the approaching and gigantic ruin of at least a stage of civilization" (III/4, 638 = 556). But sloth in the wicked sense is, according to Barth, also restlessness due to anxiety and worry (IV/2, 534f. = 473). The sin of sloth consists at its core in giving in where one instead should and must stand upright (IV/2, 452f. = 403f.). Such is the banality of evil as Hannah Arendt called it with respect to Adolf Eichmann: "The sheer thoughtlessness that predestined him to become one of the greatest criminals."[5] Barth does not smile at this sin as sheer human weakness. This sin is dangerous for the church, the society, and the state.

The third form of sin is the lie. It is different than merely telling a formal inaccuracy. And the commandment to truthfulness must not exclude any conscious deception even for the sake of a just act, as Barth wrote to Dutch citizens in 1942 in their fight against the Nazis.[6] The real lie originates in shrinking back from God's acquittal in the face of the groundlessness of sin. But it nevertheless stubbornly holds its ground because the sinner, by his lie, is giving his sin an appearance of containing truth. Deliverance from pride and sloth, therefore, is connected to deliverance from the lie. Thus the lie is "sin in its most highly developed form" (IV/3, 432 = 374). Its insidiousness consists in satisfying itself with truth in a tangled way. "The true and succulent lie has a radiant aspect of righteousness and holiness, of wisdom, excellence and prudence, of zeal, austerity and energy, yet also of patience and love for God and man" (IV/3, 504 = 438).

The second line of thought Barth connects to his doctrine of sin deals with the judgment of sin in light of God's opposition to it. Sin is thus defined as nothing, as real, and as misunderstood by humanity. These three moments in the judgment of sin are only understood when they are seen as *God's* judgment that takes place in his opposition to sin. We can only know that sin is nothing, real, and misunderstood when God tells us so. It is interesting that Barth speaks, first of all, about the nothingness of sin. He does not speak about the nothingness of sin in the sense of a general superiority of God over humanity. Sin is *nothing* because it is powerless with respect to the "validity and force of the veto" that Christ "has laid upon it . . . by the act of his life as he sacrificed and fulfilled it on the cross" (IV/2, 529 = 469). Sin's nothingness does not mean that it is nothing. Rather, it means that it cannot do anything that has not been opposed by God, who has taken the sinner's place (III/3, 346 = 305). Barth talks about the *reality* of sin only secondarily, after the nothingness of sin has been discussed. He understands sin's reality in a certain sense. Although sin is powerless with respect to God, it is powerful with respect to humans. Yet despite that God's opposition to sin is also the command of the gracious God that frees humans to rise up from their sin, humans in their sloth do that which is almost "impossible . . . has no true basis . . . cannot be deduced or explained or excused or justified" (IV/2, 462 = 411). Finally, God's opposition to our sin judges our handling of sin, which is, despite his opposition, an underestimation of sin. Apart from this, we no longer see sin as absolutely intolerable and, consequently, play it down as an excusable incident. We discover sin only in the encounter of divine opposition to it. We discover that we have evaded the knowledge of our sin by denying our existence as sinners. Barth says, "This is the sin that is blacker than any other sin" (II/2, 829 = 742).

What "punishment" now follows or what do humans get for their sin? According to Galatians 6:7, God lets humans reap what they sow (IV/3, 801f. = 700f.). But Barth does not say that one falls as a *consequence* of sin, rather he says that one falls "*in* exalting himself" in sin (IV/1, 532 = 478). He understands it as follows: "He must have it as he himself wills to have it. He must be the one he himself wills to be" (IV/2, 547 = 484). This is the damage one receives from one's sin, namely, that one must be the *doer* of his own *deed*. Act and being, according to Barth's understanding, belong together in the doctrine of Christ and the doctrine of humanity and now also in the doctrine of sin. But there is an important difference. Christology speaks, first of all, about the person of Christ in order to say that his action is the work of salvation because Christ is the Savior. But in the doctrine of sin, it is the other way around. Because a person *commits* sin, he is a *sinner* (IV/1, 449 = 405f; IV/2, 551 = 487). This means however guilty in sin one may be, one is never a free human being but a depraved one: "everyone who commits sin is a slave to sin" (John 8:34; IV/2, 560 = 495). The existence of the sinner is, nevertheless, only a threat to the one who commits sin. It is " 'only' his being in the movement *towards* death" (IV/2, 550 = 487). For in Jesus Christ, God has prevented our fall towards death. In his fall, "man has fallen to the place where God who does not and cannot fall, has humbled Himself for him in Jesus Christ" (IV/1, 531 = 478). God has thereby done what we cannot do. He has made a *distinction* between the sinner and his sin. He has hated the sinner's sin but does not cease to love the sinner (IV/1, 450 = 406).

# Questions for Reflection

1. Barth's doctrine of sin has received sharp criticism in particular. For example, according to Cornelis van Til, Barth leads people "to think that they are not sinners." There is then no heresy so "ultimately destructive of the Gospel as is the theology of Barth."[7] Or, according to Wolfhart Pannenberg, sin for Barth is "merely" a shadow within the religious action of Christian believers. Therefore, it is "not at all necessary," he says, for non-Christian humanity to have a "reversal" of human determination.[8] What are these critics directing their criticism against? What can be said about these charges? What is the essential concern about Barth's doctrine of sin? And what are its arguments?

# THE JUSTIFICATION AND SANCTIFICATION OF THE SINNER

When asked what he had against the Lutheran focus upon the doctrine of justification, Barth answered, "What I have against it is that in 1 Corinthians 1:30 I read: '. . . Christ Jesus, whom God made our wisdom, our righteousness, and sanctification and redemption.' This is a bit more than the narrow pass into which Lutheran theology . . . entered during the sixteenth century when everything was reduced to the common denominator of this concept. . . . It was disastrous that one did not first receive this: 'Jesus Christ. . .' and from there go on to Mark 2: 'Your sins are forgiven.' And then, set back on one's feet: 'Take up your bed and *go home!*'"[1]

Martin Luther saw the doctrine of justification as the decisive difference between himself and the Roman Catholic Church. Barth also says, "Without the doctrine of justification . . . there never can be any true Christian church" (IV/1, 583 = 523). But a subsequent book by Hans Küng came to the conclusion that there exists a "fundamental agreement between the theology of Barth and that of the Catholic Church."[2] Is Barth really so irenic or does Küng's claim merely cover over an existing contrast? Barth's controversial claim is "The *articulus stantis et cadentis ecclesiae* [the article by which the church stands or falls] is not the doctrine of justification as such, but its basis and culmination: the confession of *Jesus Christ*, 'in whom are hidden all the treasures of wisdom and knowledge' (Col 2:3)" (IV/1, 588 = 527). Has Barth thereby "corrected the Reformation"?[3] Or did he not remain true to his own statement?[4]

Without denying the "dignity and necessity" of the doctrine of justification, Barth resists the attempt "to allow all other questions to culminate or merge into it" (588f. = 528). The doctrine of sanctification and the calling of the Christian, each has its own dignity. This cannot be diminished even by the insight that the believer "even in his best works . . . still stands in continual need of justification before God" (IV/2, 570 = 504). Barth believes that whenever these doctrines refer to Christ, it becomes clear that they are necessary in order to speak about *him*. Barth is also concerned to say that our theology is a *theologia viatorum*, "a theology on its way to the kingdom of God." It does not have a master key to solve all questions "from the standpoint of God" (IV/1, 587 = 526). This thought invites us to be open to new evidence regarding *the extent to which "all the treasures* of wisdom and knowledge" are hidden in Christ.

To claim that the confession of *Christ* is the main article of faith is not to claim an uncertain basis for agreement. As paths separate with regard to the subject of justification, so were they already separated with regard to faith in Christ. But if this is taken seriously, then there is hope in the midst of theological conflict. Barth says, "In a theological conflict, the opponents are still *together* in Christ and therefore still within the church when it is clear that they are separated in Christ and that they contend not about the respective rights of their churches, or tendencies within their churches or only their own personal opinions, but about the right of the church against heresy, which makes this dispute necessary" (I/2, 924 = 826). But in Christ one cannot be *separated* without acknowledging that one is so *in him* who is the *peace* within conflict. The peace sought in separation can only be found in him in whom the peace is already given, even though we do not yet see it. Separation thus cannot be reinterpreted as an expression of potential variety. One must, therefore, *seek* him.

Justification is thus measured according to who Jesus Christ is, what he does and suffers for us, according to the Old and New Testament. The Bible takes up a lot of space in Barth's doctrine of justification. The backbone of this doctrine, Barth says, is "the backbone of the relationship with God even in the Old Testament" (IV/1, 592 = 531). He not only provides an exegesis here of the letter to the Galatians (711–717 = 637–642). He also places Pauline statements in the context of Old Testament passages (592f. = 531f.; 597f. = 535f.; 599f. = 537f.; 636f. = 570f.; 643–659 = 577–591; 675–678 = 605–608; 694f. = 621f.). And all this refers to Jesus Christ as the foundation of everything. "Everything that has to be regarded as the reality and truth of justification and faith and their mutual relationship begins in Him and derives from Him" (712 = 637). According to Barth, the emphasis in this matter should not be "so much upon the idea that man is justified by *faith* and not by *works* as upon the prior consideration that it is *God* and not *man* who accomplishes the justification."[5] There is nothing in a person, not even his faith or his passivity, that helps him to gain salvation. Our justification relies solely upon God in whom our faith rests. On the other hand, the grace of God in order to be pure grace must not stop human activity. This is why Barth can speak about faith as our act (IV/1, 846 = 757). He thus does not understand our sanctification as a consequence of faith but as a consequence of that *into which* we put our faith. Our sanctification has already taken place in Christ.

Barth rejects an understanding of justification that is widely spread in Protestantism that provides the basis for a "double existence" of the individual in the "static co-existence of two men . . . in which he has either simultaneously or alternately to see himself" (606 = 543; 660 = 591f.; 673 = 603f.). This suggests "double bookkeeping" in which a person on the one hand, in a "certain narcissism," rejoices in one's personal and private salvation, and on the other hand "he is subjected to other lords in a kingdom on the left as well as to the Lord Jesus Christ whose competence extends only, as we think, to the forgiveness of sins" (IV/2, 571 = 504; IV/1, 588 = 527f.). Finally, this idea raises the suspicion that justification is "a mere 'as if'" (605 = 542f.; 667 = 597). Because the confession of Christ is for Barth the basic Christian confession, he then appeals to *the* authority in whose light the true meaning of justification is disclosed. A *new* disclosure is necessary and Barth demonstrates this by Wilhelm Dilthey's provocative statement that the "entire view of life which makes up the presupposition of the Protestant doctrine of justification as the central conviction of the Reformation is over and therefore the doctrine of justification . . . no longer has any meaning for us."[6] In face of modern questions about this doctrine, Barth saw no other choice but to return to the confession of Christ and elaborate this doctrine anew in this light. How is justification to be understood in the light of Jesus Christ?

Justification is to be understood primarily as an unparalleled *act of right*. It is also an unparalleled act of grace. But it is not "merely a verbal remission" (IV/1, 666f. = 596f.) that leaves alone the wrong that has been forgiven. God does not do without his justice in this act of grace. He does not offer grace at the expense of justice. He is gracious to the sinner by doing justice to him. The pardoning of the sinner through justification thus may not fall under the suspicion of minimizing human wrong. "There is no doctrine more dangerous than the Christian doctrine of the atonement . . . if we do not consider it with this warning in view. The fact that it speaks of God making good what we have spoiled does not mean that we can call evil good (unless we would also call good evil!)" (IV/1, 74 = 70). But God makes good what we spoil. For his grace occurs in his "taking away . . . wrong and man as the doer of it" (597 = 535). It is not about "punishing" his wrong. It is about shutting off the source from which it comes (279f. = 254). This does not contradict the grace of God. "His grace would not be grace without his judgment" (546 = 490). God's judgment is *the* element in his grace that serves as the antidote against the wrong of the sinner that God never calls good. The wrong of the sinner is without grace. God's judgment of it is not without grace. It is the "redemptive fire of his love" (546 = 490). This is confirmed by the fact that justification has a second aspect: "the establishment of his (the divine) right, the introduction of the life of a new man who is righteous before God" (619 = 554). Just as the resurrection of the dead is a miracle, so the righteous act of justification is a miracle because of the grace of God. God leads a person by this miracle from wrong to right, from death to life (621 = 557; 661 = 593). This already touches upon the work of sanctification.

It is God who justifies the unrighteous. Barth goes beyond the classical doctrine and says not only that God justifies *humanity* but also that "this work of the justification of unrighteous man God also and in the first instance justifies *Himself*" (626 = 561). Barth discusses here the problem of theodicy. In doing so, he corrects the modern approach to it. Man cannot ask about a justification of God in face of all the suffering in the world without remembering that he himself is a sinner in need of justification. It is not man who justifies God in front of the forum of the throne of his justice. God justifies *himself*. But God is not so highly exalted that he avoids justifying himself. Sin nevertheless raises questions as to whether God, despite the chaos that invaded his good creation, is still its Lord and whether God chose man in vain to be his covenant partner (627f. = 562f.). For Barth, the answer lies in linking the justification of God with the justification of man. God justifies man by exposing himself to these questions. He allows the reversal that threatens his creation and his covenant to fall upon himself. In all this he surrenders "His own impassibility" of the "world of evil" judged by him (II/2, 178 = 163). He exposes himself to it in order to be exposed to the threat of his creature and his covenant. This overturns "the picture of a God who is dead because of his pure deity" (IV/1, 626 = 561).

At this point, we have to say explicitly that our justification takes place in *Jesus Christ*. Everything that has been said so far about justification has already been said with reference to him. If Jesus Christ is the main article of Christian faith, according to Barth, then this includes justification, and it follows that justification should only be discussed "in Christ" and not apart from him. *He* is our righteousness. Our righteousness is to us "always a *strange* righteousness." It is first of all true "in this *Other One*, not in us." But because he took *our* place, this is also true: "His history is as such *our* history. It is our *true* history (incomparably more direct and intimate than anything we think we know as our history). . . . In Him we are quite alone" (IV/1, 612f. = 548f.). These two sides define the concept of faith. That the individual believer, as Paul says, "lives as one who is righteous by faith to the exclusion of all works is something that he will establish and attest in his works—the particular doctrine of justification that we find in the Epistle of James" (701 = 627). For that which Christ is doing *extra nos* (outside of us) becomes an event *in nobis* (in us) (IV/4, 20 = 18) so that it now becomes true "that Christ is in the Christian" and "the Christian is in Christ" (IV/3, 629 = 547f.). *Thus* Christ is the Lord who determines them in their faith.

But does Barth not annul here the Reformation understanding of the believer as *simul iustus et peccator* (simultaneously righteous and sinner)? According to Barth, God became human in order to *separate* sin and righteousness. We should accept what Christ has accomplished in our place once and for all in faith. But the concluding stroke drawn in Christ across our old life need not constantly be drawn over it again, and the door to a new life opened to us in his resurrection does not need constantly to be opened anew (IV/1, 623 = 558). What took place through Christ affects our lives in such a way that it puts us on a *new road* and calls us to move forward. This is true for *each* step. "That which has been in Jesus Christ" is still present in him as that which has been "the wrong which is blotted out and the wrong-doer with it." But "the future will always be the past of human wrong and the human wrong-doer," just as the righteousness in a new life that he received in our place is "our future which cannot become the past again" (623 = 558). On this road we have "in every present *both* this past and this future" (639 = 573).

Barth says, finally, that through the justification of the sinner God justifies the human as *human*. Just as God according to his good will towards man justified *himself*, so he claims man *himself* and his humanity from his own self-destruction. Though God rejects the sinner, he does not reject the human. He denies the sinner because he affirms the human. This does not mean that sin is merely the outer husk of a good kernel in humans. But in justification the definition of a human is challenged by his sin. God justifies the human in such a way that he cannot lose his humanity despite his wrong deeds. But neither can he attain his humanity through his best deeds. In this sense, we have to distinguish between the humanity of man and man as the doer of his deeds. Barth calls the person distinguished from his deeds "man himself" (IV/3, 920–926 = 804–809). By justifying the sinner, *God* shows his *love* to this very human. God loves him so that "the man himself" is none other than the *human* unconditionally *loved by God*. He knows him quite well as a sinner. But he does not love him because of his sin. He opposes the human's sin because he loves him. He loves him by justifying him. This human is hidden to *us*. We can only *believe* that this human exists. But we *should* believe that others and ourselves exist as such humans against all outward "disguises"[7] by which we surround ourselves and that only make us see others and ourselves as much too obtrusive. In believing this, we affirm the distinction that God makes between our existence as humans and our existence as sinners, which is impossible for sinners to make, and we agree to live it out obediently.

Such obedience is part of sanctification. God treats us as his own and lays claim upon us so that we would confirm his claim upon our lives. Sanctification, according to Barth, is both the consequence and goal of our justification (IV/2, 575 = 508) and, at the same time, our preparation for witnessing to the gospel in the "world" on the way to God's kingdom being fulfilled (IV/3, 657 = 572f.). As justification means the gracious acceptance of the lost sinner through God, so sanctification means that God claims this same person for a new way of life. The first delineates itself from legalism, the latter from paganism. Barth emphasizes both, unmixed yet undivided. A false mixture means that one would become righteous before God because of one's own merits. A false division exists when gospel and law are set against each other. At any rate, it is not right to look first to Christians. Barth points to 1 Corinthians 1:2, Philippians 1:2, John 17:19, and Hebrews 10:10

to explain, "How much false teaching, and how many practical mistakes, would have been avoided in this matter of sanctification if in direct analogy to the doctrine of justification by faith alone we had been bold or modest enough basically and totally and definitively to give precedence and all the glory to the Holy One and not to the saints" (IV/2, 583 = 515; 585f. = 517f.).

But Christians are not sanctified because they give glory to him but rather because they "*are* already sanctified, already saints, in this One" (584 = 516). As our sanctification is already completed in him, so we have been completely delivered from all sick self-reflections and are invited to look to him. Our sanctification is our participation in his sanctity. It takes place through the invigorating power of his Holy Spirit (592 = 523), by whose power we belong to the Holy One and receive "direction" from him. We? Barth says here as well: *de iure*, "according to law," this is true for all, *de facto*, "effectively," it is true for all those who follow him (578f. = 511f.). The Holy One has a right to all people because none are annexed from him. But for the time being only some actually acknowledge his power. And they are not simply saints but, in contrast to undisturbed sinners, they are "disturbed sinners" (593 = 524). They are being sanctified. Although they are still threatened and sinners in need of forgiveness (597 = 527f.), they are nevertheless already "differentiated from the world, . . . fellow-saints with the Holy One, His people" (593 = 524). Barth emphasizes three particular things with regard to these saints.

First, "The Holy One . . . who is the active Subject of sanctification . . . exists only in the singular as *the* saints do only in the plural." Saints under the Holy One do not exist in isolation but in overcoming this isolation of their sin in *fellowship* as a holy people of saints in a holiness they receive together. All this takes place according to the Old Testament quotation in 1 Peter 2:9: "you are . . . a holy nation, God's own people" (579f. = 511f.). This leads to an understanding of the Christian congregation that Barth describes with the definition coined by the lawyer Erik Wolf: it is "brotherly Christocracy" (770 = 680). This does not merely characterize the church as a fellowship of love and feeling but as a legally binding form in which her Lord unites Christians as brothers and sisters.

Second, sanctification is particularly a battle against the sin of sloth in which a person cowers and limits himself and slumbers through life. Sanctification takes place in resistance to this perversity. The kingdom of God is "the contradiction of everyone's sloth, and especially their [the saints'] own" (593 = 524, rev.). Certainly, "how painfully we lift up ourselves." But we may and shall nevertheless, according to Hebrews 12:2, be as those: "*looking to* Jesus . . ." (emphasis added). Barth interprets this passage, "This looking to Him, not with bowed but uplifted head, is the setting up of these men. It is their . . . sanctification" (597 = 528). This is our sanctification: learning to walk with our heads erect. Its mark is not dour seriousness but joyful cheerfulness. This is not yet the future resurrection of the body, but even now a lifting up is occurring.

Third, what is the relationship of those sanctified to those around them who are still, effectively, unsanctified? Barth says that, on the one hand, sanctification means conforming to the Holy One in obedience to his "call to discipleship" (603–626 = 533–553). Paul speaks of how strict this call is in Romans 12:2: "Do not be conformed to this world." This means that following Christ takes place and has to do with "a *break* with the great self-evident factors of our environment, and therefore of the world as a whole" (625 = 552). The disciple of Christ can, therefore, become an offense to the world around him "by seeming to be strange and foolish and noxious" (617 = 545). For this reason he may have to carry a cross (689f. = 609f.). He will not then make a practice of renouncing the world, yet it should be said that, on the other hand, he will continue to turn nevertheless precisely to this "world." The people of God are "the salt of the earth" and "the light of the world" (Matt 5:13-14). "As the people created by Jesus Christ and obedient to him," his congregation is "essentially impelled to exist for God and therefore for the *world* and *men*" (IV/3, 873 = 763).

# Questions for Reflection

1. According to Gerhard Ebeling, the church "stands and falls" on justification by faith. Wilhelm Dilthey says that justification by faith is meaningless. Compare these opposing theses. What can we learn from Barth with respect to these opposing theses?

2. What is meant by the different concepts of "justification of humanity" and "justification of God"? What does Barth say about these different concepts? Is it really possible to combine them and treat them in the way he claims?

3. How can we understand the claim that those justified by God are "simultaneously justified and sinners"? What is right about this claim? Where are the problems with it? How does Barth correct this claim? Examine this claim in light of what Paul says about it in Romans 7–8.

4. Barth says that all humans are "lawfully" sanctified in Christ but that not all are "effectively" grasped by it. What is the actual difference? How can the meaning of this differentiation be understood? Why does Barth make this distinction? Do we miss out on something if we are not "effectively" sanctified?

5. The New Testament says both "you are the salt of the earth," that is, "the light of the world," and "Do not be conformed to this world." Are these sentences contradictory, such that one can take only one or the other seriously? How can both be affirmed? Does what Barth says about this make sense to you?

# THE GATHERING AND SENDING OF THE CHURCH

As previously mentioned, Barth interprets the word "church" and its significance on the basis of Mark 3:34. The Latin translation of this verse refers to Jesus' "true relatives" as those who "continue in a circle around Him" (IV/4, 41 = 37). For Barth, this is the prototype of the Christian church. This teaches observers how essential fellowship and gathering with others is to the Christian life. "To be awakened to faith and to be added to the community is one and the same thing . . . there is no legitimate private Christianity" (IV/1, 768f. = 688f.). That people are connected with each other by cultivating some common conviction certainly does not make them a church. What makes their gathering a church is only that Jesus is in their midst. In order to know what we are dealing with in this gathering of his community, we must not look to the community, but above all to him and then only from him to the community and not the other way around. Barth can speak about this in drastic terms:

> It (the church) may become a beggar, it may act like a shopkeeper, it may make itself a harlot—as has happened and still does happen, yet it is always the bride of Jesus Christ. . . . What saves it and makes it indestructible is not that it does not basically forsake Him—who can say how deeply and basically it has often enough forsaken Him and still does?—nor is it this or that good that it may be or do, but the fact that He does not forsake it, any more than Yahweh would forsake His people Israel in all His judgments. (IV/1, 772 = 691)

Barth liked to refer to Luther's interpretation of Matthew 14:24-32 regarding the church: *Fluctuat non mergitur*, "She is tossed about, but does not sink" (IV/2, 765 = 676).

Even if the church were successful as a booming religious enterprise, God would desert her if this "center" is missing by which alone she is the church. She is dead if she makes herself the center or makes something else the center. Because everything depends on this *one* center and because he really stands in her *midst*, the confession's claim that the church is *one* now becomes clear. This does not exclude a great variety of other insights, practices, and tasks. One can also distinguish between the visible and the invisible church, between the church that is still in battle here on earth and the one already fulfilled, between the people of Israel then and the church called at Pentecost now. But we need to be clear about this: in all these varieties and forms, it is not about different churches but always about the one church of God (IV/1, 746–749 = 668–671). And if there were and still are divisions, every split is "a dark mystery, a *scandal*." One who simply tries to blame the other side is not yet a "good Christian" (IV/1, 754 = 676). The only way for the church to be the one visible church is for believers, each in their own place, to struggle in repentance to be the church of *Jesus Christ*. Barth writes with respect to the relationship between Christians past and present, "The dead no less than the living have a part in the 'communion of the saints.' It is not only the living who speak and act, but their predecessors, their words and works, their history, which does not end on their departure, but . . . [it is] standing in an indissoluble relationship with the history of the present" (IV/1, 747 = 669). And he says about the relationship of the church with Israel, "There are differences which we cannot overlook. . . . But it is the *one* history, beginning there, having its center in Jesus Christ and here hastening to its culmination. It is the arch of the *one* covenant which stretches over the whole" (IV/1, 749 = 670, rev.).

In what way is the church "*holy*" according to the confession? Barth does not hesitate to say that the church "within Adamic humanity is just as unholy as that humanity, sharing its sin and guilt and standing absolutely in need of its justification" (IV/1, 767 = 687). The old saying that there is no salvation outside of the *church* should, according to Barth, much rather say that there is no salvation outside of *Christ* (769 = 688). This means that the limitations of the church are not a limitation to God's gracious and reconciling care of humanity in Christ. However, in spite of her sin, the Christian church can and must be in order in this respect: in the *knowledge* of Christ, in her *faith* in him, and in the service of the *proclamation* of his name (IV/1, 769 = 688f.). According to Barth, this is what makes the church holy, despite her neediness. Members of the church are distinguished from those outside her by this knowledge, this faith, and this service. Let us keep in mind (chapter 3) that, according to Barth, the beginning of the Christian life, namely, in baptism, must already be a mature step (IV/4, 55 = 50). This is probably what distinguishes her from Judaism, into which one normally enters through birth.

The Christian church is alive only as she has the center of her life in Christ. But there are two dangers in which she finds herself (even though she will face them both "in the name of Jesus"!): *sacralization*, in which she is immersed in a self-glorification before the world that has a different orientation than she has, or *secularization,* in which she adjusts to the methods of worldly powers and fashions (IV/2, 754–758 = 667–670). Yet she "may often be *almost* overwhelmed by the danger which threatens from without and within; but she will *never be completely* overwhelmed" (761 = 672, rev.). This is so because her Lord does not fall, "and so the church cannot fall" (764 = 675). The latter confirms that humans are not merely passive *receivers* of the divine gifts of grace. God's salvation wills and accomplishes that they are independent *partners* of God and of his action. For Barth, God's grace would not be sufficient if it did not reach its goal *here.*

In 1967, Barth said, "Today there is much ready talk . . . about *the world* which is supposed *to have come of age* in relation to God. However that may be, my own concern is rather with the man who ought to come of age in relation to God and the world, [that is,] the mature Christian and mature Christianity" (IV/4, x = ix–x). It demonstrates the greatness of God's grace that man here "is taken seriously as an independent creature of God . . . not run down and overpowered but set on his own feet . . . not put under tutelage but addressed and treated as an adult" (IV/4, 25 = 22f.). But a person is not an adult by himself. One becomes an adult as one hears about God, as one learns and always continues to learn "in the *apostles'* . . . school" (IV/1, 798 = 714f.). And even though a person may learn well, maturity in the life of a Christian is *always* reached in such *partnership.* The maturity grounded in God's grace is freedom in relation to others and among others. It is a freedom "to live in contact, solidarity . . . with God, but also with men . . . as companions in the partnership of reconciliation" (IV/3, 285 = 248, rev.).

If the grace of God extends to the maturity of all church members, it probably means that the church is alive in a host of different tasks. But the differences in these tasks should not mean the establishment of a stable arrangement of individual office bearers on the one side and a group of subordinate laity on the other. "The living Lord Jesus Christ deals directly with his living church, not indirectly, not by some sort of ordered system of representation."[1] Communities, therefore, cannot afford the contradiction "so that *on the one side* [with the laity] they cannot do enough to accommodate their concern about human arbitrariness, while *on the other side* [with the office bearers] they carelessly 'make mere flesh their strength' [Jer 17:5]." There should be in the church "no 'clergy' and no 'laity,' no simply 'teaching' church and no simply 'listening' church, because there is no member of the church who would not be or do all these at his own place."[2] "Ordained" to the ministry of the church "are all those baptized as Christians" (IV/4, 221 = 201). In place of the voice of *one* office, there needs to be a "multiplicity of Christian witness" (IV/3, 988 = 862).

The activity of the entire church in the variety of her forms of witness is necessary because the entire church gathered around the word of the Lord is at the same time also sent out. She is sent to give witness to the message she has heard. The difference between Christians and other people is not that those within the church have salvation and those outside her do not have it. The only difference is that members of the church have heard and recognized that which remains or is again hidden to others. But the community of Jesus Christ is "the human creature which is ordained by nature to exist for the other human creatures distinct from her. She . . . exists for herself only in fulfillment of this ordination. . . . She saves and maintains her own life as she commits herself to and gives herself for all other human creatures. . . . The center around which she moves 'eccentrically' is not, then, simply the world as such"—or else she would end up in fatal conformities—"but the world for which God is"—which disrupts the church's commitment to and the excess of energies she spends on her own self-preservation (IV/3, 872 = 762, rev.).

In her missionary service, the church is not imposing something unfavorable on her fellow humans, for the Word of God became *human*—not Christian (John 1:14)—and in him, Jesus Christ, God reconciled the *world* to himself (2 Cor 5: 19). This grounds the sending of the *church* to her environment. Yet this does not ground the reality of *God's* presence in the part of the world that is not churched. "On the other hand, the community of Jesus Christ has a very inadequate view of its Lord, the King of Israel who is also the King of the world, if it is not prepared to recognize that even world-occurrence outside takes place in *His* sphere and under *His* governance, or if it tries to imagine that in this occurrence we are concerned with either no God at all, or with another God, or with another will of the one God different from His gracious will demonstrated in Jesus Christ" (IV/3, 786 = 686).

The church is called to be God's witness within her own times. But she can *only* be a witness and not the mediator of salvation. She cannot bring about the self-mediating reality of the world's reconciliation with God. God brings it about. This excludes the community interacting with those who receive her witness in an overly protective way, by which she would meet them as the owner or administrator of the riches of salvation. She would then be patronizing to her fellow humans. And patronage means "the human exercise of power by men against other men." Such patronage treats others merely as grist for one's own mill (IV/3, 948, 950 = 827f., 829). In dealing properly with my fellow humans, I may much rather expect to hear "true words" from them (IV/3, 144ff. = 128–130). However, according to Barth, witness in the Christian sense of the term is discreet, "the greeting with which . . . I have to greet my neighbor, the declaration of my fellowship with one in whom I expect to find a brother of Jesus Christ and therefore my own brother. . . . A witness will not intrude on his neighbor. . . . Witness can be given only when there is respect for the freedom of the grace of God, and therefore respect for the other man who can expect nothing from me but everything from God" (I/2, 487f. = 441).

One of Barth's more surprising claims becomes clear in relation to the mission of the church: the church is sent to her fellow humans to give witness to the salvation that Christ provided for the world, which the world does not yet know. The church is, therefore, *limited* in this essential task that she has. She is not eternal. "The community exists between His coming then as the risen One and this final coming. Its time is, therefore, this between time" (IV/1, 810 = 725). During this time, the community has to proclaim what good things God has already done and, therefore, will do in Christ in word and deed and in a variety of forms of service. She will hopefully do so in an inviting way. But the community is not the end of God's ways. *This* is the goal: "The coming Jerusalem in which [Revelation 21:22] tells us there will be no more temple because the Almighty God will Himself be its temple" (826 = 739).

# Questions for Reflection

1. What does it mean that Christ is the center of his community if Jews are also counted as members of this community? In what way are Jews and Christians encompassed under the same arch of the *one* covenant? Can this be said without violating Jews or flattening out the Christian message? Is it not better to see Jews as members of a different religion? Either way, how are Christians to deal with the *first* Testament?

2. Is Barth actually taking the grace of God completely seriously when he emphasizes so strongly the maturity of all Christians? What is to be understood by the maturity of all members of the community? What does community life look like if there are supposed to be no merely teaching and no merely listening members in it? And if every Christian is "ordained," is Barth not devaluing the office of the pastor with respect to the rest of the community?

3. If the entire community is sent out to people in its surroundings, how is her mission to be carried out? What do the members of the community have to do in their workplace or outside of it? Can the community learn something from the mission work of sects in this respect? How is the mission of the Christian community different from theirs?

4. Is the difference between Christians and non-Christians really only that the former recognize what the latter have not yet recognized or no longer recognize? Is the difference not much rather that Christians have been saved through faith whereas this is not true for the nonbelievers? How can God's salvation in Christ be valid for those who have no faith in him?

CHAPTER 4.9

# THE RESURRECTION OF JESUS AND OUR HOPE

A professor of mathematical logic once asked Barth what he considered the nail on which all theology hangs. Barth answered, "The resurrection of Jesus Christ from the dead!" His friend then said, "This goes against all the laws of physics . . . and chemistry but now I understand you."[1] According to Barth, we have to say that "If there is any Christian and theological axiom, it is that Jesus Christ is risen, that He is truly risen. But this is an axiom which no one can invent. It can only be repeated on the basis of the fact that in the enlightening power of the Holy Spirit it has been previously declared to us as the central statement of the biblical witness" (IV/3, 47 = 44).

Barth had come from a theology that cast a shadow on the gospel of Easter. Friedrich Schleiermacher, Barth's spiritual father in his early years, explained, "The facts of the Resurrection [of Jesus] . . . cannot be laid down as properly constituent parts of the doctrine of His Person."[2] Schleiermacher says that this is so not because we *can* no longer believe them but because we do not *need* them. The church preserves such a picture of the personality of Jesus that is sufficient to move us to a religiously fulfilled life. However, to renounce faith in the resurrected One has serious consequences for the Christian faith. One can then no longer say in what way God meets us in this person. What we say about the resurrected One is then based on relative impressions. Faith becomes a human possibility of a religious relationship. Faith then does not see the new that God sets over against a world gone wrong. It sees itself as the inner power of humanity to adapt—either in a reforming or a conservative way—to the conditions of the world. And such a faith that suppresses the resurrected One will fill this gap with the church or Western culture in order to manage its own spiritual heritage.

Schleiermacher also wrote that if there is nevertheless among Christians a faith in the facts of the Resurrection, they "are only accepted *because they were written down*."[3] Barth became suspicious about the dogma of the dispensability of the Easter faith because he saw in it a contradiction to what is "written" in the Bible. *Therefore*, it is necessary to thoroughly rethink this matter because the Christian faith can be led astray by it. In the face of this dogma, it is the task of theology to think about the witness of Holy Scripture regarding the message of Easter. An apostle is, according to Luke, a "witness . . . to his resurrection" (Acts 1:22). Paul called himself an apostle (Gal 1:1) because he understood his encounter with Christ as an Easter story (Gal 1:16; 1 Cor 15:8). But *we* know about the resurrection of Jesus Christ only through the witnesses of the resurrection. What is a witness? Barth says that the attitude of the witness "is distinguished from the attitude of the interested spectator, or the narrating reporter, or the reflective dialectician, or the determined partisan, by the fact that when the witness speaks he is not answering a question which comes from himself but one which the judge addresses to him. And his answer will be the more exact and reliable the more . . . he allows it to be exclusively controlled by the realities which it is his duty to indicate and confirm." In the resurrection of Christ, God pronounces a judgment and calls witnesses to testify. "They are called by God in the face of all other men to be witnesses of His own action" (I/2, 913 = 817). We only understand them if we take them seriously as *witnesses—them* and not a "fact" that we have reconstructed behind them (IV/1, 377 = 341f.). To be a witness means that that which his witnesses confessed made them witnesses so that we through their witness would receive it.

They witness to us about an event in which God alone acts. No human cooperates with it (IV/1, 332ff. = 301ff.). The eyewitnesses about whom the Bible speaks only witness to the consequence of this event. But they also do not speak about their own faith. What they confess stands out despite their unbelief. But if it is about an event in which God alone acts, then we cannot grasp this event with the concept that modernity has invented, namely, the *historical* (*historische*), which means verification by the methods and "above all the tacit assumptions of modern historical scholarship" (III/2, 535 = 446). According to Barth, the Easter event cannot be classified among such "historical facts." He nevertheless insists that God's single act on Easter is not a timeless myth. It takes place in space and time among humans. It is history "which the modern historian will call 'saga' or 'legend'" (535 = 446), or "primal history" (*Urgeschichte*) or "'pre-historical' happening" (IV/1, 371 = 336), history of that kind which most of the Bible "is full of . . . and contains comparatively little 'history' (*Historie*)." But "it is sheer superstition to suppose that only things which are open to 'historical' verification can have happened in time. There may have been events that happened far more really in time than the kind of things that 'historians' as such can prove. There are good grounds for supposing that the history of the resurrection of Jesus is a pre-eminent instance of such an event" (III/2, 535 = 446, rev.), for God acts here without human cooperation in a fundamentally revolutionary and renewing way.

The apostles testify to this in *different* ways: "That is nothing to be upset about! . . . Yes, there are different traditions that can and must not be harmonized. . . . If it is about such an event as this: true life from death! . . . No wonder that the reports shake like houses in an earthquake and contradict each other!" What lack of taste "when we now come with our historical spectacles, trying to find out what the original was? You've got to be kidding: '*The* original'! In every line of the New Testament it is possible to hear amazement in everything said in face of that which is absolutely unique." The apostles speak about it "in entirely different ways . . . but they all look in the same direction."[4] We are taking these texts seriously if we allow each of them to point us in the same direction that all of them look.

Barth does not understand Easter as a historical event that is overtaken and relativized by subsequent historical events. He understands it as an eschatological event, an event of the end-times. And he understands it as the Parousia, that is, "the new coming of Jesus Christ who came before." He is "no other than the one who had come before" in his earthly life in time (IV/3, 336f. = 291f.). But he comes again in a new way. He comes in such a way that he is not bound to a limited time. And he also comes in such a way that what was hidden during his earthly life in time is now "revealed." This now coming to light as Easter is not just another date in a limited time, but it is the beginning of the eternal significance of that which happened then and there. Barth says that this is the beginning of the end-times: "In the Easter event as the commencement of the new coming of Jesus Christ in revelation of what took place in His life and death, it is also revealed that the time which is still left to the world and human history and all men can only be the last time" (340f. = 295f.). The end-times primarily demonstrate that God is reaching the goal with his creatures in history and in the giving of himself for the reconciliation of the world. The world now hears what God has done. This takes place as the life of Jesus Christ, "which has now been terminated by death but which by participation in the sovereign life of God is delivered from all past or future perishing, being made eternal by the omnipotence of the grace of God" (359 = 311f.).

What has been said thus far already implies what needs to be explained. The Easter event is, according to Barth, an event that is not bound to one specific time but encompasses all times. It is an event in which a perfect tense, a present tense, and a future tense are bound together in closest connection. They are bound together by the one Jesus Christ whom the Bible makes known as the One "who is and who was and who is to come" (Rev 1:8; cf. Heb 13:8). Barth understands this witness as follows: it is about the three forms of the one new coming of him who came before. It is, three times, about the revelation of Christ's victory over hostile powers in favor of his oppressed creatures (IV/3, 335ff. = 290ff.). The Parousia is carried out in three forms: in his Easter appearance, in his present impartation of the Holy Spirit, and in his last coming as the Author of the resurrection of the dead and as the Fulfiller of the last judgment (338 = 293). But, according to Barth, each of these three different occurrences are about the one and the same new coming of the One who came before. In these three occurrences, the return of Jesus Christ in the last days takes place. And because it is about his one return, all three forms have the same three characteristics. Each is about the total, the universal, and the definite emergence of that which has been accomplished in the reconciliation of the world with God in Jesus Christ (347 = 301).

Here are more specific explanations. The first form of the Parousia is the Easter appearances that the disciples experienced. The Parousia of Jesus does not take place only once. It has happened. It is in the perfect tense. John 1:14 says that "we *have seen* his glory (emphasis added)." Barth interprets this verse, "What the disciples came to see in the appearances of the Resurrected was . . . initially just the same as what will one day be manifest to all eyes . . . In its totality, universality and definitiveness it then passed into the reality of world-occurrence, of human existence both in detail and as a whole, of the cosmic being and life which are the presupposition and sphere of human existence. It was incorporated into this whole" (347 = 301). Whenever Christians think about the Parousia of Jesus Christ, they do not merely look to the future but primarily to the perfect tense attested by Scripture. The eschaton already *took place* in it. This happened in a first form, but it happened in such a way that Christians receive from it a glimpse and measure for that which happens *now* and that which will happen *then* in the coming of the Lord.

The second form of the Parousia is the coming of Jesus Christ through the Holy Spirit into our present. Thus he comes ever since Pentecost. It is "essential" to him to be not only in the past and the future but to be the Lord and Savior of the world today (IV/2, 703 = 622). The universal dimension of his coming again is combined here with the great commission that Jesus gave to his disciples: "Go into all the world" (Mark 16:15)! "In the Easter event is grounded the necessity of Christian mission. A Christianity with no mission to all would not be Christianity" (IV/3, 350f. = 304f.). But necessity does not mean compulsion here. It rather means that for Christianity this sending goes without saying. A church that does not engage in missionary work is not only disobedient but has forgotten its purpose. If the church is the church, it will be on the move. "It has the freedom to fulfill its duty of mission in the knowledge that its Lord has long since *preceded* it with His Word in His resurrection, and that He is always well ahead of it, so that in this respect, too, it has only to follow Him" (351f. = 305). This shapes the church's present: "He not only did bear the sin of the world, He *does bear* it. He not only *has* reconciled the world with God, but as the One who has done this, He *is* the eternal Reconciler, active and at work once and for all" (IV/1, 345 = 313).

The third form of the Parousia is Christ's return at the end of all time. This is the hope of Christians. They know that this hope is not a dream because they already know him whom they hope for. A Christian "hopes on the basis of the 'then' of His resurrection, and therefore 'now' in virtue of His presence and action in the power of the Holy Spirit" (IV/3, 1050 = 915). But the Christian still *must* hope because he for whom the Christian hopes is not yet visible. Rather, what is visible is often that which contradicts the Christian's hope. The Christian hopes in Jesus Christ—"Can he hope in Him as the coming *judge*? Yes, in Him as such . . . There can be no doubt that His judgment is the future of the whole world and therefore of the Christian, too." But "he waits for His grace which *judges*, and which cuts with pitiless severity in this judgment, he still waits for His grace. He waits for His grace, which is absolutely *free, unmerited and sovereign* in the execution of His judgment, he still waits for His grace. He waits for His righteousness but . . . for the righteousness of His grace" (1058f. = 922). God's judgment definitely precludes that *we* sit on his judgment throne. And his grace would not be pure, free grace if it were not the grace of this righteous judge. But we may have hope. We may hope that the judgment of this gracious One and the grace of this judge is our final future.

# Questions for Reflection

1. It is difficult to distinguish, linguistically, between a historical fact and history. Are you able to make this distinction between the two, which is so important to Barth for understanding the resurrection of Christ? According to him, Easter is not a historical event (*historisches Ereignis*) but an eschatological one. Again, what is the difference between these two concepts? Do you accept this understanding of Easter?

2. According to Barth, the return of Christ is perfect, present, and future, a single threefold form. How is this thesis unusual? How does he justify this thesis? Are there any good arguments against it?

3. What does the mission of the church have to do with Christ's return? If there is a connection here, what kind of understanding of the mission of the church develops from it in contrast to other views of it?

4. The final coming of Christ is, according to Barth, his coming in judgment that is, at the same time, grace. Is Barth not combining two opposing concepts here? And if he does, would God's grace not then be a terrible thing or his judgment a harmless process that ends in a "reconciliation of all"?

# NOTES

## Introduction

1. Karl Barth, *Einführung in die evangelische Theologie* (Zürich: Evangelischer Verlag, 1962), 182; ET: *Evangelical Theology: An Introduction* (New York: Holt, Rinehart and Winston, 1963), 165.

## 1: The Early Period of Barth's Theology: "God Is God"

1. Karl Barth, *Der Römerbrief*, 2nd ed. (München: Christian Kaiser Verlag, 1922; 12th ed., 1978), 314, 326, 396; ET: *The Epistle to the Romans* (Oxford: University Press 1933), 330, 342, 411.

2. Eberhard Busch, *Glaubensheiterkeit* (Neukirchen-Vluyn: Neukirchener Verlag, 1986), 43f.

3. Karl Barth, *Predigten 1907–1911*, ed. Eberhard Busch (Zürich: Theologischer Verlag Zürich). This volume in Barth's *Gesamtausgabe* is not yet in print. The following citation refers to the sermon number which Barth himself designated: 36.

4. Ibid., 51.

5. Ibid., 66.

6. Ibid., 36.

7. Ibid., 43.

8. Karl Barth, "Der christliche Glaube und die Geschichte" (1910), *Vorträge und kleinere Arbeiten, 1909–1914*, ed. Hans-Anton Drewes and Hinrich Stoevesandt (Zürich: Theologischer Verlag Zürich, 1993), 193. This essay was first published in *Schweizerische theologische Zeitschrift* 29 (1912): 1–18, 49–72. The reference above is on page 58.

9. Karl Barth, *Predigten 1907–1911*, 51, 36.

10. Ibid., 136.

11. Ibid., 62.

12. Ibid., 63.

13. Ibid., 47.

14. Ibid., 36.

15. Karl Barth, *Komm, Schöpfer Geist!* (München: Christian Kaiser Verlag, 1924), 17; ET: *Come, Holy Spirit*, trans. George W. Richards, Elmer G. Homrighausen, and Karl J. Ernst (New York: Round Table, 1934), 16.

16. Karl Barth, *Das Wort Gottes und die Theologie* (München: Christian Kaiser Verlag, 1924), 20, 28, 15; ET: *The Word of God and the Word of Man*, trans. Douglas Horton (New York: Harper Torchbooks, 1957), 24, 32, 43, rev.

17. Barth, *Der Römerbrief*, 2nd ed., 246; ET: 263–64, rev.

18. Barth, *Der Römerbrief*, 2nd ed., 118; ET: 141–42, rev.

19. Barth, *Der Römerbrief*, 2nd ed., 65; ET: 91.

20. Barth, *Der Römerbrief*, 2nd ed., 220; ET: 238, rev.

21. Barth, *Der Römerbrief*, 2nd ed., 68; ET: 94, rev.

22. Barth, *Der Römerbrief*, 2nd ed., 72; ET: 97, rev.

23. Barth, *Der Römerbrief*, 2nd ed., 62; ET: 88, rev.

24. Barth, *Der Römerbrief*, 2nd ed., 73; ET: 98, rev.

25. Barth, *Der Römerbrief*, 2nd ed., 73; ET: 98, rev.

26. Barth, *Der Römerbrief*, 2nd ed., 18; ET: 42, rev.

27. Barth, *Der Römerbrief*, 2nd ed., 242; ET: 260, rev.

28. Hans Urs von Balthasar, *Karl Barth: Darstellung und Deutung seiner Theologie* (Köln, Germany: Jacob Hegner, 1951), 92; ET: *The Theology of Karl Barth*, trans. John Drury (San Francisco: Holt, Rinehart and Winston, 1971), 84.

29. Barth, *Der Römerbrief*, 2nd ed., 196; ET: 215, rev.

30. Barth, *Der Römerbrief*, 2nd ed., 423; ET: 437, rev.

# 2: The Rise of the Confessing Church: "The One Word of God"

1. Karl Barth, *Die Briefe des Jahres 1933*, ed. Eberhard Busch (Zürich: Theologischer Verlag Zürich, 2004), 177f., 157.

2. Karl Barth, "Die Barmer Theologische Erklärung" in K. D. Schmidt, *Die Bekenntnisse und grundsätzlichen Äusserungen zur Kirchenfrage*, II (1935): section 42, 91–98. ET: "The Theological Declaration of Barmen" in *The Church's Confession Under Hitler*, trans. Arthur C. Cochrane (Philadelphia: Westminster Press, 1962), 237–42. Also found in *The Book of Confessions* of the Presbyterian Church (USA).

3. Karl Barth, *Gottes Wille und unsere Wünsche*, Theologisches Existenz heute! 7 (München: Christian Kaiser Verlag, 1934), 6.

4. Karl Barth, *Theologische Fragen und Antworten*, Gesammelte Vorträge 3 (Zollikon, Switzerland: Evangelischer Verlag, 1957), 132f.

5. Karl Barth, *Die Kirche Jesu Christi*, Theologisches Existenz heute! 5 (München: Christian Kaiser Verlag, 1933), 13–18.

6. Eberhard Busch, *Unter dem Bogen des einen Bundes: Karl Barth und die Juden 1933–1945* (Neukirchen-Vluyn, Germany: Neukirchener Verlag, 1996), 173.

7. Karl Barth, *Gotteserkenntnis und Gottesdienst* (Zollikon, Switzerland: Evangelischer Verlag, 1938), 203ff.; ET: *The Knowledge of God and the Service of God According to the Teach-*

*ing of the Reformation: Recalling the Scottish Confession of 1560*, trans. James L. M. Haire and Ian Henderson (London: Hodder and Stoughton, 1938), 222ff.

8. Karl Barth, *Theologische Existenz heute: Schriftenreihe* (München: Christian Kaiser Verlag, 1933), 3; ET: *Theological Existence Today! A Plea for Theological Freedom*, trans. Richard Birch Hoyle (London: Hodder and Stoughton, 1933), 9–10.

9. Reformationstag 1933. *Dokumente der Begegnung Karl Barths mit dem Pfarrernotbund in Berlin*, ed. and introduction by Eberhard Busch (Zürich: Theologischer Verlag Zürich, 1998), 106.

10. Karl Barth, *Eine Schweizer Stimme, 1938–1945* (Zollikon, Switzerland: Evangelischer Verlag, 1945), 180, 185, 192, 184.

11. Barth, *Theologische Fragen und Antworten*, 133.

# 3: The Theologian in the Struggles and Hopes of His Time: "Not Only Your Loved Ones!"

1. Not yet in print.

2. Karl Barth, *Einführung in die evangelische Theologie* (Zürich: Evangelischer Verlag Zürich, 1962), 182; ET: *Evangelical Theology: An Introduction*, trans. Grover Foley (New York: Holt, Rinehart and Winston, 1963), 165.

3. "Friss Vogel oder stirb" is a colloquial expression that is roughly equivalent to "Like it or lump it."—Trans. note.

4. Karl Barth, *Briefe, 1961–1968* (Zürich: Theologischer Verlag Zürich, 1975), 474.

5. Eberhard Busch, *Karl Barths Lebenslauf* (München: Christian Kaiser Verlag, 1975), 394; ET: *Karl Barth: His Life from Letters and Autobiographical Texts*, trans. John Bowden (Philadelphia: Fortress Press, 1976), 379–80.

6. Barth, *Einführung in die evangelische Theologie*, 18; ET: 12.

7. Karl Barth, *Christliche Gemeinde im Wechsel der Staatsordnungen: Dokumente einer Ungarnreise, 1948* (Zollikon, Switzerland: Evangelischer Verlag, 1948), 12; ET: "The Christian Community in the Midst of Political Change: Documents of a Hungarian Journey" in *Against the Stream: Shorter Post-War Writings 1946–1952*, ed. Ronald G. Smith, trans. Stanley Godman (London: SCM, 1954), 60.

8. Barth, *Christliche Gemeinde*, 30; ET: 78.

9. Barth, *Christliche Gemeinde*, 65; ET: 113.

10. Barth, *Christliche Gemeinde*, 69; FT: 116

11. Karl Barth, *Offene Briefe 1945–1968*, ed. Diether Koch (Zürich: Theologischer Verlag Zürich, 1984), 220.

12. *Amsterdamer Dokumente* (Bielefeld, 1948), 146.

13. *Evanston Dokumente*, ed. F. Lupsen (Witten, 1954), 55.

14. Hans Urs von Balthasar, *Karl Barth: Darstellung und Deutung seiner Theologie* (Köln, Germany: Jacob Hegner, 1951); ET: *The Theology of Karl Barth*, trans. John Drury (San Francisco: Holt, Rinehart and Winston, 1971).

15. Hans Küng, *Rechtfertigung: Die Lehre Karl Barths und eine katholische Besinnung* (Einsiedeln, Switzerland: Johannes Verlag, 1957); ET: *Justification: The Doctrine of Karl Barth and a Catholic Reflection*, trans. Thomas Collins, Edmund Tolk, and David Granskou (Philadelphia: Westminster Press, 1964).

16. Karl Barth, *Gespräche 1959–1962*, ed. Eberhard Busch (Zürich: Theologischer Verlag Zürich, 1995), 279.


# 4: The *Church Dogmatics*: "To Think Is to Think After"

## 4.1: The Faith That Seeks Understanding

1. Karl Barth, *Unterricht in der christlichen Religion 1924, I* (Zürich: Theologischer Verlag Zürich, 1985), 35; ET: *The Göttingen Dogmatics: Instruction in the Christian Religion I*, trans. Geoffrey Bromiley (Grand Rapids, Mich.: William B. Eerdmans, 1991), 28, rev.

2. Karl Barth, *Das Wort Gottes und die Theologie* (München: Christian Kaiser Verlag, 1925), 175; ET: *The Word of God and the Word of Man*, trans. Douglas Horton (Gloucester, Mass.: Peter Smith, 1978), 212.

3. Karl Barth, "Der christliche Glaube und die Geschichte" in *Schweizerische theologische Zeitschrift* 29 (1912): 69f.

4. Karl Barth, *Predigten 1914* (Zürich: Theologischer Verlag Zürich, 1974), 523.

5. Karl Barth, *Die Theologie und die Kirche* (München: Christian Kaiser Verlag, 1928), 227f.; ET: *Theology and Church*, trans. Louise Pettibone Smith (New York: Harper and Bros., 1962), 228f.

6. Karl Barth, *Nein! Antwort am Emil Bruner*, Theologische Existenz heute! 14 (München: Christian Kaiser Verlag, 1934), 38f.; ET: *Natural Theology*, trans. Peter Fraenkel (London: Geoffrey Bless, 1946), 101f.

7. Barth, *Die Theologie und die Kirche* 221; ET: 223, rev.

8. Karl Barth, *Das christliche Leben* (Zürich: Theologischer Verlag Zürich, 1976), 30, 206; ET: *The Christian Life*, trans. Geoffrey Bromiley (Grand Rapids, Mich.: William B. Eerdmans, 1981), 21, 125.

9. Barth, *Das christliche Leben*, 192; ET: 118.

10. Barth, *Die Theologie und die Kirche*, 212–39; ET: 217–37.

11. Kornelis Heiko Miskotte, *Über Karl Barths Kirchliche Dogmatik. Kleine Präludien und Phantasien*, TEH NF 89 (München: Kaiser Verlag, 1961), 41.

12. Karl Barth, *Fides Quaerens Intellectum* (München: Christian Kaiser Verlag, 1931), 26; ET: *Anselm: Fides Quaerens Intellectum*, trans. Ian Robertson (Richmond, Va.: John Knox Press, 1960), 27.

13. Barth, *Fides Quaerens Intellectum*, 94; ET: 92, rev.


## 4.2: The Freedom of the Triune God

1. Otto Weber, *Karl Barths Kirchliche Dogmatik. Ein einführender Bericht*, 10th ed. (Neukirchen-Vluyn: Neukirchener Verlag, 1984), 22; ET: *Karl Barth's Church Dogmatics: An Introductory Report*, trans. Arthur C. Cochrane (Philadelphia: Westminster Press, 1953), 33.

2. Karl Barth, *Homiletik: Wesen und Vorbereitung der Predigt* (Zürich: Theologischer Verlag Zürich, 1970), 101; ET: *Homiletics*, trans. Geoffrey Bromiley and Donald Daniels (Louisville: Westminster John Knox Press, 1991), 122, rev.

# 4.3: The Covenant of Grace Made with Israel and Fulfilled in Jesus Christ

1. Karl Barth, *Unterricht in der christlichen Religion 1924/1925*, II (Zürich: Theologischer Verlag Zürich, 1990), 392.

# 4.4: The External Basis of the Covenant and the Internal Basis of Creation

1. Cf. Jürgen Moltmann, "Schöpfung, Bund und Herrlichkeit," *Zeitschrift für dialektische Theologie* 3 (1987): 212.
2. Karl Barth, *Nein! Antwort am Emil Brunner*, Theologische Existenz heute! 14 (München: Christian Kaiser Verlag, 1934), 14; ET: *Natural Theology*, trans. Peter Fraenkel (London: Geoffrey Bless, 1946), 77, rev.
3. Karl Barth, *Die Theologie und die Kirche* (München: Christian Kaiser Verlag, 1928), 211; ET: *Theology and Church*, trans. Louise Pettibone Smith (New York: Harper & Row, 1962), 215.
4. Friedrich Schleiermacher, *Der christliche Glaube*, vol. 1, ed. Martin Redeker (Berlin: Walter de Gruyter & Co., 1960), 26; ET: *The Christian Faith*, trans. H. R. Mackintosh (Edinburgh, Scotland: T&T Clark, 1928), 16.
5. As it is taught by Paul Tillich, *Systematische Theologie*, Vol. 1, 2nd ed. (Stuttgart: Evangelisches Verlagswerk, 1956): 294–98; ET: *Systematic Theology*, I (Chicago: University of Chicago, 1951).

# 4.5: The Content of the Covenant-Law and the Form of the Covenant Promise

1. Eberhard Jüngel, "Zum Verhältnis von Kirche und Staat nach Karl Barth," *Zeitschrift für Theologie und Kirche* 6 (1986): 103.
2. Karl Barth, *Evangelium und Gesetz*, Theologische Existenz heute! 32 (München: Christian Kaiser Verlag, 1935), 11; ET: "Gospel and Law," in *Community, State, and Church: Three Essays* (Gloucester, Mass., 1968), 80.
3. Barth, *Evangelium und Gesetz*, 17; ET: 85.
4. Karl Barth, *Fürchte dich nicht!* (München: Christian Kaiser Verlag, 1949), 97.
5. Barth, *Evangelium und Gesetz*, 17; ET: 85.

# 4.6: The Exposure of Sin in Light of Its Overcoming

1. Karl Barth, *Die christliche Lehre nach dem Heidelberger Katechismus* (Zollikon, Switzerland: Evangelischer Verlag, 1948), 38; ET: *The Heidelberg Catechism for Today*, trans. Shirley Guthrie (Richmond, Va.: John Knox Press, 1964), 44; cf. III/3, 397 = 345, IV/2, 496f. = 440f.

2. Gerhard Ebeling, *Lutherstudien*, vol. 3 (Tübingen, Germany: J. C. B. Mohr [Paul Siebeck], 1985), 564.

3. Karl Barth, *Das christliche Leben* (Zürich: Theologischer Verlag Zürich, 1976), 35f.; ET: *The Christian Life*, trans. Geoffrey Bromiley (Grand Rapids, Mich.: William B. Eerdmans, 1981), 24f., rev.

4. Barth, *Das christliche Leben*, 359; ET: 212.

5. Hannah Arendt, *Eichmann in Jerusalem. Ein Bericht von der Banalität des Bösen* (München: Piper, 1964), 16. ET: *Eichmann in Jerusalem: A Report on the Banality of Evil* (New York: Penguin Classics, 2006).

6. Karl Barth, *Eine Schweizer Stimme, 1938–1945* (Zollikon, Switzerland: Evangelischer Verlag, 1945), 248f.

7. Cornelius Van Til, "Has Karl Barth Become Orthodox?" *Westminster Theological Journal* 16 (1954), 81.

8. Wolfhart Pannenberg, *Anthropologie in theologischer Perspektive* (Göttingen: Vandenhoeck & Ruprecht, 1983), 88; ET: *Anthropology in Theological Perspective*, trans. Matthew J. O'Connell (Philadelphia: Westminster Press, 1985), 92.

# 4.7: The Justification and Sanctification of the Sinner

1. Karl Barth, *Gespräche 1963*, ed. Eberhard Busch (Zürich: Theologischer Verlag Zürich, 2005), 258f.

2. Hans Küng, *Rechtfertigung: Die Lehre Karl Barths und eine katholische Besinnung* (Einsiedeln, Switzerland: Johannes Verlag, 1957), 274; ET: *Justification: The Doctrine of Karl Barth and a Catholic Reflection*, trans. Thomas Collins, Edmund Tolk, and David Granskou (Philadelphia: Westminster Press, 1964), 282.

3. Gerhard Ebeling, *Karl Barths Ringen mit Luther*, Luther-Studien, Vol. 3 (Tübingen, Germany: Mohr-Siebeck, 1985), 497–509.

4. Eberhard Jüngel, "Um Gottes willen—Klarheit! Kritische Bemerkungen zur Verharmlosung des kriteriologischen Rechtfertigungsartikels—aus Anlass einer ökumenischen, Gemeinsamen Erklärung zur Rechtfertigungslehre," *ZThK* 94 (1997): 394–405; and the same, *Das Evangelium von der Rechtfertigung des Gottlosen als Zentrum des christlichen Glaubens: eine theologische Studie in ökumenischer Absicht*, 3rd ed. (Tübingen, Germany: Mohr Siebeck, 1999).

5. Karl Barth, *Das christliche Leben* (Zürich: Theologischer Verlag Zürich, 1976), 466f.; ET: *The Christian Life*, trans. Geoffrey Bromiley (Grand Rapids, Mich.: William B. Eerdmans, 1981), 269.

6. Wilhelm Dilthey, *Das Erlebnis und die Dichtung. Lessing, Goethe, Novalis, Hölderlin*, 4th ed. (Leipzig, Germany: Reclam-Verlag, 1913), 151; ET: *Poetry and Experience: Rudolf A. Makkreel and Frithjof Rodi* (Princeton: Princeton University Press, 1985).

7. Karl Barth, *Das Wort Gottes und die Theologie* (München: Christian Kaiser Verlag, 1924), 200; ET: *The Word of God and the Word of Man*, trans. Douglas Horton (New York: Harper Torchbooks, 1957), 251, rev.

# 4.8: The Gathering and Sending of the Church

1. Karl Barth, *Die Schrift und die Kirche*, Theologische Studien 22 (Zollikon, Switzerland: Zürich Evangelischer Verlag, 1947), 37.

2. Ibid., 37, 42f., 39.

# 4.9: The Resurrection of Jesus and Our Hope

1. Karl Barth, *Gespräche 1964–1968*, ed. Eberhard Busch (Zurich: Theologischer Verlag Zürich, 1997), 47f.

2. Friedrich Schleiermacher, *Der christliche Glaube*, vol. 2, ed. Martin Redeker (Berlin: Walter de Gruyter & Co., 1960), 84; ET: *The Christian Faith*, trans. H. R. Mackintosh (Edinburgh, Scotland: T&T Clark, 1928), 417.

3. Schleiermacher, *Der christliche Glaube*, vol. 2, 87; ET: 420, rev. Italics added.

4. Barth, *Gespräche 1964–1968*, 43

# BIBLIOGRAPHY

## Works of Karl Barth

Barth, Karl. "Die Barmer Theologische Erklärung" in K. D. Schmidt, *Die Bekenntnisse und grund sätzlichen Äusserungen zur Kirchenfrage*, II (1935): section 42, 91–98. "The Theological Declaration of Barmen" in *The Church's Confession Under Hitler*. Trans. Arthur C. Cochrane (Philadelphia: Westminster Press, 1962), 237–42. Also found in *The Book of Confessions* of the Presbyterian Church (USA).

———. *Die Briefe des Jahres 1933*. Ed. Eberhard Busch. Zürich: Theologischer Verlag Zürich, 2004.

———. *Christliche Gemeinde im Wechsel der Staatsordnungen: Dokumente einer Ungarnreise, 1948*. Zollikon, Switzerland: Evangelischer Verlag, 1948. Trans. Stanley Godman under the title "The Christian Community in the Midst of Political Change: Documents of a Hungarian Journey" in *Against the Stream: Shorter Post-War Writings 1946–1952*. Ed. Ronald G. Smith. London: SCM, 1954, 51–124.

———. *Die christliche Leben. Die Kirchliche Dogmatik IV, 4, Fragmente aus dem Nachlaß Vorlesungen 1959–1961*. Eds. Hans-Anton Drewes and Eberhard Jüngel. Zürich: Theologischer Verlag Zürich, 1976. Trans. Geoffrey Bromiley under the title *The Christian Life [Church Dogmatics IV/4]*. Grand Rapids, Mich.: William B. Eerdmans, 1981.

———. *Evangelium und Gesetz*. Theologische Existenz heute! 32. München: Christian Kaiser Verlag, 1935. Trans. James Strathearn McNab under the title "Gospel and Law" in *God, Grace and Gospel*. Edinburgh, Scotland: Oliver and Boyd, 1959.

———. *Fürchte dich nicht! Predigten aus den Jahren 1934 bis 1948*, München: Christian Kaiser Verlag, 1949.

———. *Gottes Wille und unsere Wünsche*. Theologisches Existenz heute! 7. München: Christian Kaiser Verlag, 1934.

———. *Gotteserkenntnis und Gottesdienst*. Zollikon, Switzerland: Evangelischer Verlag, 1938. Trans. James L. M. Haire and Ian Henderson under the title *The Knowledge of God and the Service of God According to the Teaching of the Reformation: Recalling the Scottish Confession of 1560*. London: Hodder and Stoughton, 1938.

———. *Kirchliche Dogmatik*. Zollikon, Switzerland: Evangelischer Verlag, 1932–1967. Trans. Geoffrey Bromiley under the title *Church Dogmatics*. Edinburgh, Scotland: T&T Clark, 1956–1975.

———. *Offene Briefe 1945-1968*. Ed. Diether Koch. Zürich: Theologischer Verlag Zürich, 1984.

———. *Predigt über Röm. 15, 5–13*, in Karl Barth, *Die Kirche Jesu Christi*, Theologische Existenz heute! 5. München: Christian Kaiser Verlag .

———. *Reformationstag 1933*. Ed. Eberhard Busch. Zürich: Theologischer Verlag Zürich, 1998.

———. *Der Römerbrief, 1922/23*. Zürich: Evangelischer Verlag, 1954. Trans. Edwyn Hoskyns from the sixth edition under the title *The Epistle to the Romans*. London: Oxford University Press, 1933.

———. *Eine Schweizer Stimme, 1938–1945*. Zollikon, Switzerland: Evangelischer Verlag, 1945.

———. *Theologische Existenz heute: Schriftenreihe*. Zwischen den Zeiten 2. München: Christian Kaiser Verlag, 1933. Trans. Richard Birch under the title *Theological Existence Today! A Plea For Theological Freedom*. London: Hodder and Stoughton, 1933.

———. *Theologische Fragen und Antworten*. Gesammelte Vorträge 3. Zollikon, Switzerland: Evangelischer Verlag, 1957.

———. *Das Wort Gottes und die Theologie*. München: Christian Kaiser Verlag, 1924. Trans. Douglas Horton under the title *The Word of God and the Word of Man*. New York: Harper Torchbooks, 1957.

Barth, Karl, and Eduard Thurneysen. *Komm, Schöpfer Geist! Predigten*. München: Christian Kaiser Verlag 1924. Trans. George W. Richards, Elmer G. Homrighausen, and Karl J. Ernst under the title *Come, Holy Spirit*. New York: Round Table, 1934.

# Secondary Literature

Biggar, Nigel. *The Hastening That Waits: Karl Barth's Ethics*. Oxford: Clarendon Press, 1993.

Burnett, Richard E. *Karl Barth's Theological Exegesis: The Hermeneutical Principles of the* Römerbrief *Period*. Grand Rapids, Mich.: William B. Eerdmans, 2004.

Busch, Eberhard. *Glaubensheiterkeit: Karl Barth*. Neukirchen-Vluyn, Germany: Neukirchener Verlag, 1986.

————. *Karl Barth's Lebenslauf.* München: Christian Kaiser Verlag, 1975. Trans. John Bowden under the title *Karl Barth: His Life from Letters and Autobiographical Texts.* Philadelphia: Fortress Press, 1976.

————. *Unter dem Bogen des einen Bundes, Karl Barth und die Juden.* Neukirchen-Vluyn, Germany: Neukirchener Verlag, 1996.

Ford, David F. *Barth and God's Story: Biblical Narrative and the Theological Method of Karl Barth in the Church Dogmatics.* Frankfurt am Main: Verlag Peter Lang, 1981.

Hunsinger, George. *Disruptive Grace: Studies in the Theology of Karl Barth.* Grand Rapids, Mich.: William B. Eerdmans, 2000.

————. *How To Read Karl Barth: The Shape of his Theology.* New York: Oxford University Press, 1991.

Jüngel, Eberhard. *Barth-Studien.* Zürich: Benziger Verlag; Gütersloh; Gütersloher Verlagshaus Gerd Mohn, 1982. Trans. Garrett E. Paul under the title *Karl Barth: A Theological Legacy.* Philadelphia: Westminster Press, 1986.

————. *Gottes Sein Ist Im Werden.* Tübingen, Germany: J. C. B. Mohr (Paul Siebeck), 1965. Translated under the title *Doctrine of the Trinity: The Being of God Is in Becoming.* Grand Rapids, Mich.: William B. Eerdmans, 1976.

————. "Zum Verhältnis von Kirche und Staat nach Karl Barth." In *Zeitschrift für Theologie und Kirche* 83/6 (1986): 76–135.

Köckert, Heidelore, and Wolf Krötke, eds. *Theologie als Christologie. Zum Werk und Leben Karl Barths. Ein Symposium.* Berlin: Evangelische Verlagsanstalt, 1988.

Marquardt, Friedrich-Wilhelm. *Theologie und Sozialismus: Das Beispiel Karl Barths.* 3rd ed. München: Christian Kaiser Verlag, 1980.

McCormack, Bruce L. *Karl Barth's Critically Realistic Dialectical Theology.* Oxford: Clarendon Press, 1995.

McDowell, John C. *Hope in Barth's Eschatology. Interrogations and Transformations Beyond Tragedy.* Burlington, Vt.: Ashgate, 2000.

Moltmann, Jürgen. "Schöpfung, Bund und Herrlichkeit. Zur Diskussion über Barths Schöpfungslehre" in *Zeitschrift für dialektische Theologie* 3 (1987): 191–214.

von Balthasar, Hans Urs. *Karl Barth. Darstellung und Deutung seiner Theologie.* 2nd ed. Köln, Germany: Jakob Hegner, 1961. Trans. John Drury under the title *The Theology of Karl Barth.* San Francisco: Holt, Rinehart and Winston, 1971.

Webster, John. *Barth's Moral Theology: Human Action in Barth's Thought.* Edinburgh, Scotland: T&T Clark, 1998.